WHAT IT MEANS TO BE YOU

BIRU PANDA

ISBN 979-888546066-8

What It Means To Be You: A Mindmap Of Your Soul

Birupakshya P. Panda is the author of two books, who lives in Bhubaneswar, India. This book is about mindfulness, understanding oneself, and self-discovery that falls under the motivational genre. He intends to describe what it means to be you as a unique person.

For more updates, you can follow him on Facebook (https://www.facebook.com/biru.pandaBTG770.99) or Instagram(@revospelledbackwards) or mail him at: birupanda9@gmail.com

Contents

Contents

Foreword

To my friends who made me think deeply about the origin of human nature that inspired this book idea, thank you.

To my parents who supported me in my journey.

Note To All Readers

To all the readers who picked this book, may your journey for self-discovery be everlastingly unique.

Prologue

Prometheus and Epimetheus were responsible for the creation of mankind. Back then, the humans didn't possess the ability to create fire on Earth. The Gods kept the gift of fire forbidden for the humans. With fire, they could cook and keep themselves warm, but without it, they were all just suffering.

Prometheus, the son of Zeus, was a compassionate man who took pity on mankind and the state humans were in on Earth. He requested his father to give fire to mankind; however, Zeus refused to grant humans the gift of fire. To foster the development of his creations, Prometheus promised to steal the sacred fire and give it to humanity.

Prometheus knew he wouldn't go unpunished by the Gods. He advised his brother, Epimetheus, "my misfortune will not be enough to tackle Zeus's wrath. Be careful of Zeus and his plans for humankind. With that, our creation will always be safe."

Epimetheus welcomed his brother's advice and he agreed to always stay on his guard and look out for mankind. Soon after that, Prometheus was chained by the Gods for all eternity to suffer. But just as he had predicted, Zeus devised a plan against Epimetheus and humanity.

The supreme God ordered Hephaestus to nurture the first mortal woman. The crafty God created the most graceful of all creatures. She was introduced to the Gods, who granted her different gifts. From Aphrodite she received the capacity for deep emotion, from Hermes she gained mastery over language, Athena gave her the gift of fine craftsmanship and attention to detail and Hermes gave her name, Pandora. Finally, Zeus granted Pandora the trait of curiosity. Zeus ordered Hermes to take Pandora to Epimetheus on Earth.

Back on Earth, Epimetheus had fallen in love with Pandora. He was so dazed by her unsurmountable beauty that he forgot his brother's advice, 'to be careful of Zeus's plan for mankind and to stay on guard'. Epimetheus welcomed Pandora to his palace where they lived together happily.

One fine day, Mercury, the messenger of the Gods, arrived with a mysterious box. He asked Pandora and her husband, Epimetheus, to safeguard it while he was away. However, Mercury warned her not to open the box under any circumstances. The contents of the box were not meant to be seen by the mortal eyes.

Pandora wondered what was inside the box since the box itself was already stunning. All the time she wondered what was inside the box. Could it be full of shining jewels, robes or diamonds? When Epimetheus was away and no one was around, Pandora would go near the box and run fingers over the polished wood of the box. Sometimes she was convinced she heard voices whispering and the box itself rattled inside as if straining to be free and opened.

Over time, Pandora became more and more obsessed with the box. It seemed there was a force beyond her control that drew her to the contents. Her curiosity made the box echo her name louder and louder to open the box. One day she could bear it no longer. She thought, if she opened the box, all her questions would be answered, her curiosity would be satisfied and she would be able to take her mind off it forever.

With that, she decided to open the box. With the first crack of the lid, the box burst open. A powerful pressure pushed Pandora away as a black mist escaped from the box. Zeus had filled the box with all kinds of evils; misery, greed, envy, hatred, pain, disease, hunger, poverty, war and the other evils that escaped from the box that Prometheus had not nurtured in mankind.

Until that moment, mankind was pure and lived in a golden age. There were no needs, no conflicts, no pain or no suffering. It was a world of pure happiness. But the box bought all sorts of evil that would plague humanity. Envy, cruelty, and suffering were now a part of mankind.

Pandora tried closing the box but by the time she could reach it, it was too late. Every evil had come out of the box. However, Pandora heard another whisper coming out of the box. This was not the eerie whispering of the evils but her light tinkling that seemed to ease her anguish. When she once again lifted the lid and peered in, a warm beam of light rose out and fluttered away. As she watched it flickering in the wake of the evil she had unleashed, Pandora's pain was eased.

It was Hope, hidden among the evils inside the box. Hope gives humans strength, not to give up when facing evils and obstacles that afflict them. Pandora knew that opening the box was irreversible but alongside the strife, she would set hope forth to temper its effect.

—

"It is only during one's weakest moments that one sees hope."

CHAPTER ONE

The Consciousness

Let's start the book with hope and see what we do to feel a fraction of it in our life. We'll slowly move down to our topic. What comes to your mind when you hear hope? Well, I'll tell you what I feel. The feeling that comes when an awful situation is about to turn good. The stressful event that breaks you down but the feeling that keeps you going. The unending agony after a heartbreak that I think will go on forever but eventually, it doesn't have that power over me to make me feel that way. You might have noticed how hope is related to dreadful and unlucky occurrences.

Hope appears in many ways however, for hope to surface in one's life, there has to be an unfavored situation where the person undergoing a hardship breaks one's spirit of motivation. Hope arises from within to replace that blown fire that once burned with passion. Hope is an optimistic state of mind or feeling that believes it can replenish the art of overcoming something.

We often think that Hope is that light at the end of the

tunnel that makes us breathe a sigh of relief, but it's not about the light as much as the thought of unending suffering about to end. That is why, even though you've walked half the tunnel in darkness, you feel delighted to walk the rest half when you see the light. Hope is not a destination, it's a part of your journey.

Now one might say that hope is delusional. It grants you a superior optimistic feeling that makes you believe you can do superficial things, which you've never done, quite easily. And that one person might be right. I started this book with the hope that I will finish it in a month, and that motivation faded after a few weeks. But hope is never a constant factor after all. It comes and goes. Like I had mentioned, it is during one's weakest moment that they see hope in front of them. Hope is much more than a feeling; it makes you want to overcome numerous upcoming challenges. When you feel hope, you are actively busy doing things that previously felt bothersome to you. It is the new light of your life, a new motivation like starting something fresh, that you feel free and unbothered to do things without a single thought of worry.

While having hope and finding optimism is good, I want to address a topic just adjacent to this: toxic positivity. Since hope is a motivating factor and the two words are often used together, we try to find new ways to keep ourselves motivated. However, these backfires when we try to turn every bad outcome to make it seem good. Like, your toxic positivity is an obsession with positive thinking. It is the belief that all people should have a positive mindset especially when someone is undergoing a tragic experience. Forcing toxic positivity leads to suppressing negative emotions and demeaning your emotions. It can also lead to the pressure of being happy when you are devastated because they take everything to be positive.

Finding motivation or hope is hard and at most times random or rare, but forcing positivity especially just after a bad experience is not acknowledging your natural emotions. Burying emotions or masking them can lead to outbursts at certain times.

When something bad happens, such as losing your job, people tell you to "just stay positive" or "look on the bright side." While such comments are often meant to be sympathetic, they can also be a way of shutting down anything you might want to say about what you are experiencing. When you express disappointment or sadness, someone tells you that "happiness is a choice." This suggests that if you are feeling negative emotions, then it's your fault for not "choosing" to be happy.

Toxic positivity leads to avoiding or masking authentic human emotion. If you want to feel motivated and full of hope, then taking every negative occurrence as a positive one is not the answer. Toxic positivity is an avoidance mechanism. It allows them to sidestep emotional situations that might make them feel uncomfortable. But sometimes we turn these same ideas on ourselves, internalizing these toxic ideas. When we feel complex emotions, we then dismiss and deny them, never accepting them completely. It allows us to avoid feeling things that might be painful, but it also denies us the ability to face challenging feelings that can ultimately lead to growth and deeper insight.

How defense mechanisms lead to a false sense of hope:

Defense mechanisms are psychological strategies people use to separate themselves from unpleasant events, actions, or thoughts such as guilt or shame. These provide a way to dodge the unpleasant series of emotional reactions, leading them to think they have a hope of escaping reality again and again when they're uncomfortable and don't wish to deal with them. Defense mechanisms generate a false sense of hope since they created these mechanisms due to past tragic situations where they had lost all hope and decided to shun their emotional aspects. We all use defense mechanisms, consciously or unconsciously.

This book is a mind map to all possible directions, where hope leads to, where we lose it, why we create a false sense of our identity unconsciously and why we often feel low and demotivated. To cover this, I have to go over the different aspects, defense mechanisms, algorithms of unconscious actions. This book is more than just about hope. It's about understanding oneself and unveiling your mind.

These are some of the common defense mechanisms we use/have used in our lives:

1. **Denial:** It occurs when you refuse to accept reality or facts. You block external events or circumstances from your mind so that you don't have to deal with the emotional impact. It creates a false sense of hope that nothing has changed, or to be precise, nothing "has to" change by denying the painful feelings or events, thus blocking external events from your awareness. Many people use

denial in their everyday lives to avoid dealing with painful feelings or areas of their life they don't wish to admit. For example, a student may refuse to recognise their obvious lack of preparedness for an exam or you may refuse to watch the season finale of your favourite show because you want to live in the denial that it will not end.

2. **Repression**: Unsavoury thoughts, painful memories, or irrational beliefs can upset you. Instead of facing them, you may unconsciously choose to hide them in hopes of forgetting about them entirely. This is different from denial because you're trying to hide or bury them instead of denying them. It is for the hope that masking these particular memories would lead to a better life. Since you've hidden them, there's no need to worry about facing them again. However, that backfires when they are faced with a similar situation and they have to face it ultimately.

3. **Projection**: It's a psychological defense mechanism in which an individual attributes unwanted thoughts, feelings and motives onto another person. For instance, you might hate someone, but your inner voice tells you that such hatred is unacceptable. You can 'solve' the problem by believing that they hate you. Someone might be cheating on you, however, they accuse you of cheating instead because they're projecting their guilt unto you. They have lost hope that the other person (you) carries the same guilt as you, and hence it backfires when they self-sabotage it back to them assuming things that are not true or accusing people who are in the right.

4. **Displacement**: It's the redirection of an impulse (usually aggression) onto a powerless substitute target. Someone

who is frustrated by their superiors may go home and kick a person, beat up someone or yell at someone, even though they had nothing to do with what happened at their workplace. Neither of these people are the target of their strong emotions, but reacting to them is likely less problematic than reacting to their boss. This again creates a false sense of hope under the pretense that this is a step forward to make things right.

Defense mechanisms cause a false sense of hope because the things that led to this moment made you feel helpless to an extent that you had to deny or shun your emotions, direct them towards someone or self-sabotage it. This continues in a repeated cycle that seems to be going on and on. Day in and day out, you wonder if your life will ever be motivating or full of hope again. These mechanisms may help create a pretense of a happy situation or help you avoid reality but here's the thing: a journey of a motivating life is always authentic. It begins with true intentions, not masking half your emotions. The reason we are so devoid of hope is that at some time we gave it our all but it ended devastatingly bad and since then it's been an endless loop of restless emotions that you're not even aware of but trying your best to avoid and bury them. Sure, ignoring that strange and complex emotion that nags you every alternative day is better than actually facing it and letting it trouble you, right? No. The answer is no.

As you know, we can view consciousness as three distinct levels: the conscious, the subconscious (or preconscious), and the unconscious. This was proposed by Sigmund Freud.

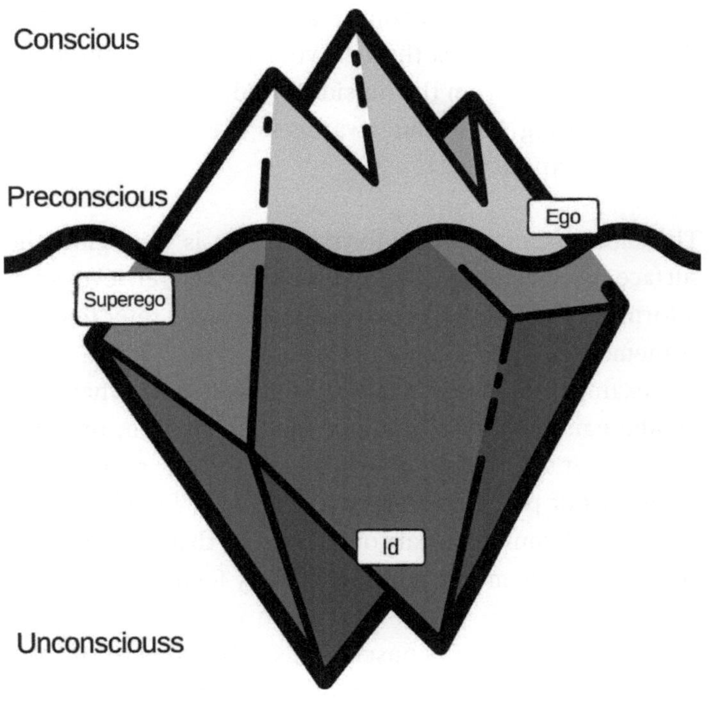

The first level of consciousness is known as the conscious state, and this refers to the immediate awareness that you are experiencing as you read this. The conscious mind consists of what we are aware of at any given point in time. It includes the things that we are thinking about right now, like your name, or address or your favourite color or where you parked your car. If we're aware of it, then it is in the conscious mind.

For example, at this moment you may be consciously aware

of the information you're reading, the sound of the music you're listening to, or a conversation you're having. All of the thoughts that pass through your mind, the sensations and perceptions from the outside world, and the memories that you bring into your awareness are all part of that conscious experience.

The subconscious holds information that is just below the surface of awareness. An individual can retrieve such information with relative ease, and we usually refer to these as memories.

For example, if someone asked you right now what your middle name was, you would be able to recall it, or when your father's birthday was or when it last rained. The memories of past experiences live in what Freud referred to as the subconscious part of our minds, that we might not be aware of one moment, and then fully focus on the next.

The final level of consciousness is known as the unconscious. This is made up of thoughts, memories, and primitive/instinctual desires that are buried deep within ourselves, far below our conscious awareness. These mostly consist of our repressed memories; memories so ghastly haunting and terrible that you had so choice but to forcefully forget them. Even though we're not aware of their existence, they have a significant influence on our behavior.

Although our behaviors tend to indicate the unconscious forces driving them, we can't readily access the information which is stored in the unconscious mind. Throughout our childhood, we gathered many different memories and experiences that formed the beliefs, fears and insecurities that we carry today. However, we cannot recall most of these memories. They are unconscious forces that drive our behaviors.

For example, things in your unconscious that might be forgotten include negative experiences from your past or a traumatic event that you pushed out of your subconscious to the unconscious. There might be some life experiences or thoughts that are too threatening for some people to fully acknowledge and are therefore repressed those thoughts/memories that now reside in the unconscious.

Now, if we go back to the topic of defense mechanisms, denial is an unconscious response to deny reality. It is said that the denied information lurks around your subconscious for a few days or weeks until it resurfaces again. This is because denial is the first step of coping with a tragic event. First, you deny that someone close to you is now your ex-friend. You have not even come to the fact that you're no longer friends. In fact, you feel like nothing has changed and hence no need to panic. But then suddenly after a few days, it gets to you. It hits you that you're no longer close and that realisation shooks you to the core. After all, denial is the first step of loss.

During repression, you try to erase memories of your terrible past occurrences. This is also used to cope. However when you repress memories or try to erase them, what you're doing is putting those painful conscious thoughts in your unconscious section of the mind. Over the years, everything you wanted to forget and move on from but couldn't, is accumulated in there. This section consists of all your fears, restless memories, traumatic events that you never want to remember again, insecurities, embarrassing situations which were so cringed you couldn't bear thinking about it again, hurtful occurrences and so on.

The unconscious mind is a storehouse for everything we have been conditioned to, told by authority, experienced emotionally and much more; it is also a large part of what we may term 'our belief' which has been formed over many years by the former set of experiences. It also sets up our habits in the way we respond in situations and our general behavior.

So, from another viewpoint, the unconscious mind represents the software that runs in the background of a computer, one that is not directly interacting with the outside world. For example, when we have an active conversation while driving, our mind is focused on listening and speaking, yet we continue to control the vehicle quite well "unconsciously", even taking the right turns and stopping as necessary. Routine tasks are generally handled in a rather unconscious manner, such as how we chew food, sit or get up, walk or climb stairs.

Our conscious mind is a very small part of our personality. Most of what we are are hidden out of reach in the unconscious part of the mind. Most of our actions, the way we react, talk, behave, think are in accordance with our unconscious mind. It's because we can only be aware of the conscious mind and not the unconscious section.

Most of what we go through in our life, emotions, beliefs, feelings and impulses deep within are not available to us at a conscious level. Most of us what influenced us, most of what made us, ourselves, and gave us our personality is our unconscious mind. That's why you always tend to figure out why am I the way I am; it was due to your unconscious values or triggers that shaped the way you are today.

The unconscious mind is a reserve of feelings, thoughts, urges and memories that are out of our conscious awareness, which contains contents that are unacceptable or unpleasant like the feelings of pain, anxiety or conflict.

The last part is the subconscious. This is the part of us that we reach if prompted but it's not in our active conscious. It's right below the surface but still hidden somewhat unless you search for it.

You can probably notice some things right now, the feeling of your feet on the floor or the weight of your clothes on your body or even pain somewhere in the body. Is this conscious or subconscious? Well, when you feel it, recognize it and are aware of it, it becomes conscious. Recognising something is the essence of being conscious of it. So, if you have the intention of doing something that you recognise you can do it quite easily, such as go and eat a sandwich because you're hungry or talk to a friend because you want to. We all have the ability to consciously choose our life.

If I want to do something, I would use my conscious mind to organise myself to do the task. I can put one foot in front of the other to walk, I can choose to call a friend or choose to take a particular job or even choose to be with particular people in my life.

However, the conscious mind is only concerned with actively doing things, it has no stored information.

Our memory is so deep and large that things that happened to us when we were young are completely forgotten now up until the age of four or six. We may remember a few bits and pieces but basically, all those memories are now stories in the subconscious mind because they do not serve any immediate purpose. We live our lives forgetting about 90% of the activities we did every day. When we're outside and listen to a point number being readout, we can hold that data consciously for about 10 seconds before it starts to fade.

In reality, we drift in and out of consciousness all the time. So we don't realise how many decisions we make subconsciously. Now, what if you were asked to strip naked and walk through a mall? There's no way, right? We can understand how uncomfortable this would make us feel yet the idea of us being uncomfortable is purely based on our experiences. Our entire subconscious would list reasons after reasons for not doing it. We would feel physical reactions to this, such as sweating, nervousness, panic, fear or embarrassment. Well, that is your subconscious making sure that we follow its code of conduct. The idea in our subconscious mind is a catalogue of experiences that told us that this is the way to deal with this.

The subconscious is there to run programs from your learned experiences. It remembers how to walk, how to sit, how to do everything. The subconscious mind doesn't forget anything. So, when it has both good practices and bad practices, it'll run the one that is the most well-rehearsed.

The inspiration can be explained as a form of a deeper subconscious. The deeper subconscious is the part of ourselves that has the ability to know more about the situation than we do. To hear the deeper mind speak, we need to be very consciously relaxed and in the zone. When we allow ourselves to work from this deeper conscious, we are truly working from the heart. When we are following our heart, we are truly following our abilities and are able to do almost everything we want.

However, to have inspiration all the time is quite difficult. When we lock into that amazing flow of energy (or inspiration), we can create amazing things but when we can't we often try to struggle to get back in that phase. But when we can't get back in there, our conscious mind attempts to take us back there by willing it and pushing it. However, this backfires and it makes things worse. We find out that we are trying to do something so badly that before we were able to do it wonderfully. Here's the thing, the conscious mind has very little processing power to accomplish complex tasks. It only has the ability to guide the ship in the right direction.

When we find ourselves not inspired, but following mindless subconscious behaviours from our past that no longer serve us, we need to use the conscious mind, to wake up and look into our behaviour and decide at the moment a new way to think about things that is more beneficial. So, all those ideas set in place years ago, drilled in by your fourth-grade teacher or by your parents to be a good child still hold true today. Each time you had a conscious experience, it soon became a subconscious memory. And the more impact each of these experiences had, whether good or bad, the more they stuck in your subconscious mind.

The important thing to remember is that your behaviour is still dictated by those experiences in your past. Generally, the learning is for your higher good but if a parent told you, that you are not good at maths, that it's not your "thing", they may have meant for not to be bothered by it and focus on the other subjects, but you may have interpreted it as a negative thing, a negative aspect of your character when it probably wasn't the case.

—

"You may live wherever you're staying now for a few years. You have to change houses in a few decades. But your mind, you live there forever. Make sure it's a nice place to stay in."

CHAPTER TWO

PATTERNS OF THE MIND

The experiences in the past that we have focused on have become habitual. And sometimes it doesn't even have to be our experiences. It could be the people in our lives that we looked up to as role models. If the role models in our lives are upset with life, angry, negative, then in many cases we can adopt that persona almost entirely. The behaviour of the people around us can tell us who we are if we don't have any other references. Sometimes our adult behaviour can basically be a complete remodeling of people that we have known in our lives.

One of the popular examples is the story of that teacher who wasn't afraid of spiders when he was a child. But once he became an adult and he came to know that his parent had a fear of spiders, they adopted that fear unconsciously in adulthood. It was baffling for this individual became he wasn't scared of the spider as a child. But he eventually realised that it's the fact that they had adopted the adult role in their adult life. Once he became an adult, he had to adapt to the adult role and so the fear also came with it.

We are constantly seeking information about ourselves, we have may not have been abused, we may have just seen who we are through the people around us. We may just have felt that we are not usually able to get what we want, so we think it's not for us.

The well-known saying, "show me your friends and I'll show you your future" is very true when it comes to the subconscious mind. The subconscious mind is always looking for references in our surroundings even though we have unlimited potential in reality. In order to make a jump outside of what is expected of us, it requires a monumental leap from the conscious mind to be able to change behaviours. Getting out of this expectation is hard. It requires a drastic change before a significant change is able to occur.

Once the conscious mind has settled down on a conclusion about life, it is absorbed down in the vast subconscious as a program to be called up to when that information is required. Now, this program runs without any conscious awareness since this happens in the subconscious. Now in a situation where we have to deal with new friends, our mind accesses the file called "how to deal with new friends" which may have been based on how you saw your adult parents deal with people or could have based on how you were treated when you got ignored at a party one time, as it was an event that shook you up.

So, when we face challenges in our adult life that require us to behave in a better way, the house of cards that our mind is set on, doesn't easily change. If you're asked to give a speech but you had experiences where adults were nervous or you were told that your words don't matter, and you took it to heart, that people didn't need to hear what you had to say, then talking becomes difficult in adult life. When the spotlight is on you, the subconscious catalogue is being vigorously checked, "what is the most prominent data that will dictate how to handle the present situation".

The subconscious might be cross-checking with other experiences of doubt or failure and conclude in a microsecond that can or can't do it well. But sometimes a positive nudge at the moment can rekindle the other memories of success in the subconscious. Now a belief in yourself and speaking more confidently can be stored as a new conscious thought that is allowing the subconscious mind to question whether or not the assumption is true or false. This new conscious feeling is so powerful, like a renewed enthusiasm and it has new current proof to back it up. It is the feeling of new belief in oneself.

Skydivers feel this euphoria all the time. At the moment when you're in the plane and you decide you're going to jump, this shakes the subconscious so much that the subconscious starts to question everything and it thinks, maybe this is a new way of experiencing life.

When you feel like you've never realised how powerful you are, this is an amazing realisation, however, if the person doubts themselves, if they're practiced self-doubt in their subconscious, the feeling of confidence at the moment is quickly thrown away and replaced by the feelings of panic and paranoia. These physical reactions are a subconscious way of altering you that there's danger ahead, so at the moment you have two choices. You can use the conscious mind and step your way through with an open eye and open mind, hoping that we can do things the way we want to or we can allow ourselves to be pulled back to the old patterns of behaviour which are very practiced and routined.

When the mind is clear and relaxed, you can use your conscious mind's imagination to direct your subconscious. But if we look at our current negative feelings and experiences, we can rewrite subconscious programs into positive experiences by seeing them in the present and re-understanding who we are. So we come to a realisation that panic and fear are the same as excitement and euphoria, just on the other side of it.

If you face your face and troubles that have been troubling you and change the behaviours that have been holding you back, this is where the subconscious is rewritten. The subconscious is a series of programs that are stored and remembered over a long period of time. But using the conscious mind, in the present to stay aware and recognising your patterns and behaviours and saying at the moment, "even though I've done this in the past, I no longer do this now", the conscious mind can rewrite the subconscious mind in a heartbeat. This is how a tragic event from the past is healed by allowing it to become a conscious decision to try again and open to how you feel.

Any tragic events from the past able to be healed by allowing emotions to be naturally processed, by bringing the pain into the conscious mind and releasing it. A boiling kettle sits there steaming away, building up but if you don't let out the steam, which is your emotions, it'll be boiling away with increasing intensity. You'll get more outbursts, and physical symbols that will build up and up and further in your life, if you're denying or repressing a hurtful or tragic event that wants to get out, if you let out the steam bit by bit at a time, eventually it'll run out of steam and then you can use your heart and mind to make the decisions that you like. But with a boiling kettle that is about to burst, it'll be difficult for anyone to behave perfectly. Your friends could be asking you, "what happened?", but the moment you do try to let out that feeling, people don't like the way you behave because you're letting out too much of the steam at the same time. Your kettle has been boiling for so long that you just can't seem to control yourself anymore. This is an evidence that your kettle has been boiling for so long that it needs a safe way to let off steam, bit by bit so that you don't find yourself pushed back again against society. You have to consciously decide how to rewrite your subconscious.

Sometimes if you just acknowledge how you feel, the bad feeling doesn't have that power over you anymore. If you make the point of making your conscious mind set an intention for what you expect to happen in life, the subconscious has no choice but to follow that decision. That is how you set your vibrations. We'll talk about vibrations in the next chapters.

Now let's come to the last part of this chapter: Id, ego and superego, the three segments as theorized by Sigmund Freud.

The Id is basically the childish and impulsive part of you

that just does what it wants, and it wants things intensely and doesn't think about the consequences. The id operates on a pleasure principle, which essentially means what it sounds like, which is that it's always seeking to try to increase pleasure and decrease pain.

Now, for another example, let's say you come home and you find to your delight that your roommate has baked a cake. Your id would think 'Oh! I want that cake right now! That looks delicious!' You know your roommate's not going to be happy if you eat it, so first, you eat a little piece of the corner, and then you have to cut yourself a slice so it doesn't look disgusting, and then soon enough you've eaten the whole thing; it's gone.

How did you manage to eat the whole cake? Blame your id for taking over. That's what your id aims to do in life. It wants you to eat whole cakes because it wants you to increase pleasure. Cakes are going to make you feel good - why not eat the whole thing? Now, what it also wants to do is decrease pain. So let's say you wake up the next morning and you think, 'Oh no, I just ate a whole cake. That's bad, maybe I'll get some exercise.' You think to yourself about how you will go hiking in the mountains all day, and you tell yourself, 'Alright, let's get some exercise!' No, your id says, 'That's not gonna happen; that's gonna hurt. We don't want to do that.' So if you're id-driven, you'd eat the whole cake and then you would not go hiking the next day to burn off the calories. That's the pleasure principle.

Now, we usually don't eat whole cakes and lay on the couch all day every day. What helps to control the rampaging id? There is another part of your personality that's mainly unconscious, and it's called the superego. The superego is the part of you that's super judgmental and moralizing and is always trying to get you to behave in a socially appropriate way. Now let's see what the superego would do if you come home and you find the cake.

If the superego is in charge, you wouldn't eat the cake at all. You'd still think it looks delicious and want to eat it, but the superego would say, 'No, it's my roommate's cake. I'm not going eat this cake!' Remember, the superego wants you to behave morally and appropriately, and it's not that socially appropriate to eat other people's baked goods.

But, let's imagine that your id takes over, so you do eat the cake. The same thing happens: you eat a little bit, you eat a little bit more, and somehow you end up eating it all. But now your superego jumps back into action. What happens now that you have already eaten the cake? You're going to feel guilt. Your superego makes you feel guilty when you do things that are not socially appropriate.

If your superego is in control again, you would certainly go jogging, but you would also apologize to your roommate and bake them a new cake, maybe an even better one than before. The superego controls our sense of right and wrong. We feel bad when we do wrong things, and we feel good when we do right things, and that's what the superego controls, your moral compass.

So, Id is like the devil sitting on our shoulders, telling us to do or get things that our instincts or impulses want immediately. The most example is of a baby who cries when he's hungry regardless of the fact that his parents are super tired. The baby wants immediate gratification through good and attention regardless of the burden on his parents. The superego is like an angel sitting on your other shoulder who has morals, who knows what is right and wrong and what is socially acceptable. It works according to rules and norms.

And the third part is the Ego. It is our conscious self. The ego is who we think we are. It has the ability to make decisions. The ego works on the reality principle. It is like a mediator who tries to satisfy both Id and Superego in a realistic way.

Suppose you have an assignment to complete due tomorrow. Now the Id is based on immediate gratification so when you start studying, you'll have thoughts like, "this is way too boring, why am I even doing this?". The Id will pressure you to engage in something pleasurable, like watching a movie or going on social media, anything that brings immediate gratification. Then the Superego is based on morals and principles and so it'll give you thoughts like, "doing my homework is the right thing to do. This is important for my class". The Superego will reward you for doing your assignment by making you feel like a good student.

Between the Id and Superego, the Ego functions of the reality principle and will come up with a realistic solution to satisfy both. The Ego will find a compromise by analysing both sides and giving you thoughts like, "I really want to watch that movie but I can't leave my assignments incomplete. So, I'll complete this first and if I'm bored I will go to social media for a break. But it's important that I complete it by tonight, that's my goal now."

Changing your state of mind by satisfying your Id

So, sometimes you follow the Id more and sometimes you follow your Superego more. Some people have a pattern of following their Id on most occasions and since Id is related to the short term things that brings you joy, this is what leads you to addiction or the formation of a habit you do not want. You start to eat more to change your state of mind because you can satisfy your Id. Superego usually includes the long terms things that seem hardships, like the good feeling you get after completing your assignment or doing your workout.

Changing your state of mind is easy and we do it unconsciously every day. Let's say, you're feeling low and you order something to eat or browse social media for a few minutes and immediately you feel better. This is where you change your state of mind, but repeatedly doing this leads to the formation of a habit. Since Id is based on immediate gratification, hence the tasks have a "less work and more pleasure" principle. You order something to eat, which requires a tap of some fingers or browse social media, which again takes a few seconds to do, and in return the reward for it is immense. The food makes you feel amazing and the posts on Instagram make you laugh producing an immense amount of dopamine for a low work task.

Now, Superego habits take longer to stick, since it's based on hardships and sticking to your disciplined rules. Like, studying requires focus and more hardship, and the joy you get in the end is not immediate. You need patience for

Superego tasks to finish since they are "long work and less pleasure" tasks.

If we're solely talking about comfort zones, it means working to satisfy your Id needs. If you always have a habit or made it a goal to satisfy the Id and not much of the Superego, then you might be stuck in your comfort zone for too long and unable to get out of it to the outside world. Superego tasks take more effort and sacrifice than Id tasks. Hence the habit formation due to Id is considered as something that can change your state of mind immediately. That's worthwhile in moderation but not as an addiction. If you have any addictions, small or big, including overeating or mindlessly scrolling through your phone, then it's an indication that you prefer Id over your Superego and you keep repeating it until it's time to do it again.

A wise person knows when to use Superego for making decisions and improving and when to use Id to calm down and take a break. You can replace your old bad habits with new ones but it'll be hard since your old habits were based on "less work and more pleasure". But here's the thing, you can't replace those habits with new productive ones immediately without an intermediary in between. Like, you can't replace the habit of scrolling through social media with studying or something productive immediately. Think of the tasks that have a moderate working period and a good, different reward. Maybe something like reading a book. Starting your journey with a task like that, that doesn't have an immediate reward but is doable is a good start and promotes the Superego side of you. It doesn't build overnight and you'll feel the doubts and a whisper from your Id that says, "quit this long task and scroll social media and get your reward immediately".

As much tempting as it is, the reward system in your mind is designed for you so you can improve and evolve with age. If you always base your reward system based on Id tasks, you might get the reward soon but the longer tasks that take a while to complete and have a lot of challenges in between to complete is what makes growth possible. Easy tasks are a good way of relaxing and getting dopamine in a whiff but you cage yourself in your comfort zone because of it.

It is said that a habit takes about 21 days to stick. But if you're an Id-driven individual, this might take longer.

Change is an essential factor and circumstances make you see the other side of it. If the subconscious mind can be rewritten, then so can the habits and morals that made you, you. Your morals might say, do not take risks if you can complete tasks easily. Well, it's time to add hardships in your equations because you are forbidding growth by listening to only your Id.

But that is why the Ego exists. Ego is the middleman between the both and hence you become the person who can see yourself objectively from both sides. You are your own savior by knowing who you are.

If you know what you lack and if you know what you need, then you're quite literally the strongest person.

By knowing your inferior habits and weaknesses, you discover and accept the whole of yourself. Every voice in your head that is based on craving the things you don't have becomes something you already know, and not something you would waste forming a first good impression for. If you know yourself for who you are, you can differentiate between the constructive and destructive criticism that people offer about you or your work. If people say words that aren't true, it is because you, yourself, know that it is not true. Knowing yourself doesn't depend on external validations anymore. You have the ability to decide consciously about the choices in front of you because you have acknowledged every thought, part of you and there is nothing to hold you back. You are truly free from yourself because your mind isn't working against you anymore.

Every confusing choice is a battle between your Id and Superego. If you know when to prefer one over the other, life becomes a little easier.

You may live wherever you're staying now for a few years. You have to change houses in a few decades. But your mind, you live there forever. Make sure it's a nice place to stay in.

—

"It is not length of life, but depth of life."

- Ralph Waldo Emerson

CHAPTER THREE

SUBLIMATION

Sublimation is a defense mechanism where socially unacceptable impulses or idealisations are unconsciously transformed into socially acceptable actions or behaviour, resulting in a long-term conversion of the initial impulse.

Whenever an individual is faced with certain thoughts, feelings or emotions that are conflicting with societal norms, it generates a lot of stress, anxiety or guilt. Since all of this is against the moral value, our mind generates a safer way to execute these feelings. This different way of channelising the same thoughts, feelings and emotions is done in a very socially acceptable manner. Thus, this reduces the anxiety or guilt that people experience. But this happens at the level of the unconscious, so the person is not aware of it.

Let me give you an example- an individual who has a lot of suppressed anger grows up to become a professional wrestler where it's socially acceptable to fight. A dancer who didn't succeed in the entertainment Industry becomes a dance instructor instead.

Sigmund Freud called this process Sublimation. It was an idea that came to him when he was reading the book, "The Harz Journey", by the poet Heinrich Heine. In it, Heine mentioned talked about the legendary German Surgeon Johann Friedrich who was extremely selfish and sadistic as a boy, loving to cut off the tails of stray dogs for sheer twisted pleasure. But then, as an adult, had matured into a profoundly selfless and brilliant surgeon, who made some marvelous discoveries in the fields of reconstructive and plastic surgery. Freud felt that this evolution, from a person who had sadistically used a knife to wound, to one who nobly used it to men was no mere coincidence. Freud believed that what was at play belonged to a widespread pattern of behaviour whereby an early harmful or shocking drive gives rise to precisely its opposite.

This desire for compensation lays at the heart of many greatest achievements in the arts, politics and science. So a great policeman might at an unconscious level, be defending themselves against certain of their illegal wishes, and a politician committed to the plight of the poor might be sublimating an early experience of raging greed.

In an essay on Leonardo Da Vinci, Freud presented the claim that Da Vinci had been an extremely sexually active child, who had then sublimated his sexuality into scientific research and art. As Freud put it, the forbidden desire for sexual pleasure had turned him into a huge honorable and powerful general urge to know.

All of us started as babies. In that state, we only wanted immediate pleasure and satisfaction. Our drives in their initial form couldn't work out for us and that had to be surrendered. We believed that if we didn't get all we wanted at once, it would be a catastrophe and we would die. That would explain the shrieking and wailing of infants in a tantrum. We thought the world revolved around us and we couldn't be generous to others and yet most of us turned into healthy adults by managing to substitute our original narcissistic aims for more ethical and fruitful ones.

We're never quite done with sublimation. We continue to be frustrated in what we want, continually we encounter people for whom we would love to have sexual desires for but mustn't, and yet rather than this energy going nowhere we have an ability to use our frustration to power other things: creative endeavors, scientific breakthroughs, care for the loved ones. Under its guidance, envy can turn into effort, egoism into a capacity for gratitude and appreciation, rejection into a film or a novel. We can turn our disappointments into more productive tasks, and grow up to not be embittered or shut down, but paradoxically energized by some of our greatest underlying sorrows.

Defense mechanisms protect the ego from non socially acceptable urges, thoughts and impulses by keeping them out of conscious awareness. So, defense mechanisms are normal and operate in the unconscious mind. Sublimation is considered as a mature defense mechanism and it's sometimes as positive. Submission takes these socially acceptable urges and coverts to socially positive behaviour and this change can be long term and can affect someone's career choice or what types of hobbies they engage in or what type of groups they're active in their life

So, one of the beliefs is that sublimation has a long-term

effect and it started because of these unsatisfactory unacceptable urges. The thing with sublimation is that the original thoughts and urges are congruent with the positive behavior. So, there are a number of urges that come up in the unconscious mind, aggression, anxiety, despair, sexual urges and greed, for example, and the idea with sublimation is that the conversion from negative to positive would be congruent.

So, for example, if the original urge was aggression, the positive outcome could be when an individual becomes a professional athlete and involves themselves in contact sports. If the original urge was sexual in nature, typically it is converted into creative energy, so somebody becomes a painter, a poem or a musician. So this congruence is a key part of sublimation.

Sublimation, as is was theorised, is in the unconscious mind. So, if something is in someone's conscious awareness, they're thinking of it right now. The subconscious contains information that you have access to but you're not thinking about it right now. Those thoughts can move into the conscious mind but only if something prompts it internally or externally. For example, if I ask you what was the name of your 10th grade teacher, it's likely that you can recall that information, so that would move that piece of information from your subconscious to conscious mind. If I ask you what your unacceptable social urges are, you won't be able to move that thought from your unconscious mind to your conscious mind. By definition, these urges are unconscious and they can't be retrieved. And this makes reading the defense mechanisms including sublimation very difficult.

Sublimation is closely related to learned behavioural patterns and we can use this in a good way to improve our approach to life. With this, the section of defense mechanisms and conscious mind comes to an end. I'll move to the next topic of the emotional spectrum and knowing your vibrations.

—

"The good and the bad thing about life is that it changes."

CHAPTER FOUR

VIBRATIONS OF THE EMOTIONAL SPECTRUM

According to string theory, every single atom, molecule, each bond between atoms, the universe, our body, earth, all the stars and galaxies are all in constant vibrations. They all vibrate at certain frequencies. It also says everything in the universe is made up of these extremely small one-dimensional vibrating objects called strings. It's the vibrational state of the string which is responsible for the mass, charge and other properties of matter. These strings are the smallest thing in the universe.

Since all the things are made up of these tiny vibrating strings, it means everything present in the universe vibrates at some frequency. Our whole universe vibrates at a frequency of 432 Hz and our home planet at a frequency of 7.83 Hz. This is the natural frequency of Earth, also known as the Schuman Resonance. The Schuman Resonance protects all living creatures on Earth. This is the reason why astronauts carry Schuman Resonance generators in space to keep them mentally and physically fit.

You might have noticed how our mood changes according to the type of music we listen to. We may feel happy, feel, sad or other types of emotions based on the song we're listening. Certain frequencies can change our moods and physical health. For example, if you hear a low frequency of around 19 Hz you'll start to feel fear, although humans are unable to hear such frequencies as it is out of the audible range of the human ear. But still, frequencies around 19 Hz will produce feelings of anxiety and fear without anyone being able to hear it. In a similar way, you'll feel relaxed and calm in presence of 432 Hz frequency. Not only this, but this frequency has many healing effects on your mind and body. This shows how our body reacts to different frequencies.

There is a specific frequency associated with a particular emotion. You can see the chart below to refer to the same. Higher frequencies mean higher vibrations which correspond to a high energy state. In the chart, you can see the good emotions have higher frequencies while bad emotions have lower frequencies. In the state of enlightenment, the frequency is highest which is more than 700 Hz.

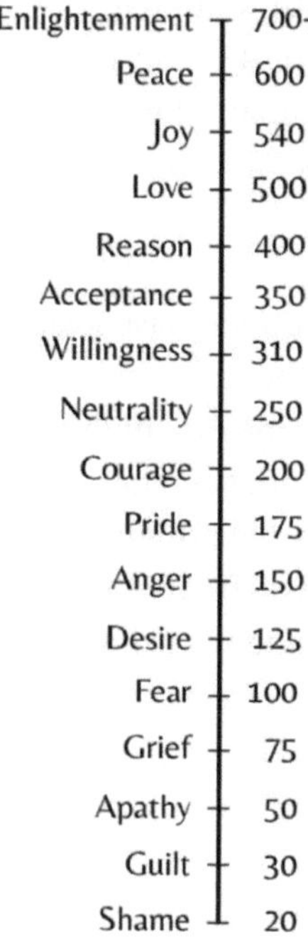

At the highest levels of frequencies like 700 Hz or more, our mind enters into a state of super-consciousness. Super-consciousness is a blissful state of self-realisation. This ego-less state is beyond the conscious and subconscious states of mind.

This chart is also called the Chart of Consciousness or the Chart of Emotional Spectrum. We have the bottom levels of consciousness which is shame, fear and guilt. Eventually, we see the level of consciousness called Neutrality. If we move a bit up we have Reasoning, which is the understanding of the mind and the intellect, and then the level of consciousness of love. Above that, we have Joy, peace and finally enlightenment.

As we go through our life experiences and as we shift our level of consciousness (or shift our vibrations), we resonate with different realities to different levels of consciousness. All the levels on the chart, there are different times in your life when we align with different emotions, different states of consciousness. But what we must become aware of is, how we are feeling the vibrational level we are at while we are intending to manifest something into our life because this is what a lot of people do: people will intend to manifest something into their life feeling anger, lack, shame guilt, feeling like they're not worthy. They're trying to manifest something into their life and so they try to do so, they're emphasizing that they don't already have what they're trying to experiment with. So, what they're doing is they're feeling the lack, that I'm to going to attract something from over there into my life, but there are different paradigms.

Let's refer to the whole chart in terms of LC-MC-HC (Lower Consciousness- Middle Consciousness - Higher Consciousness). Now let's take a look at Lower Consciousness Manifestation, saying things like "I, really, want that", "how amazing world it be for me to have that" as if things are put on a pedestal. And the more we desire that is the more resistance we feel and in order to get it, this is what we think we need to work really hard, I need to do everything I can to reach there, we can maybe find other people who can give it to us. Now, I'm not talking down to it, but what I'm saying is just be aware that's the level that you are at right now, that wanting it and giving it a lot of importance and anything we give a lot of importance to we create resistance around. The more I say I really want that, vibrationally I'm saying that I really currently don't have that. That might be how we are thinking of ourselves, that may be where are currently vibrationally but the key is understanding that that's not just who we are. That is just one perspective that we have.

Questions and thoughts like "It'll be really cool if I had that, I wonder if someone can give me a solution to all my problems, how do I attract this specific person, how do I get my Ex back", are coming from a place of lower consciousness. Don't think of Lower, middle and higher consciousness are good, bad or middle. It's not about being in a good or bad state, it's more about realising and being aware of where that energy is coming from.

So, first, we become aware of the lower emotions we're feeling, the shame, fear, guilt, anger, or thoughts like "why do other people have it and I don't". If you're mad at other people for having it, then it's a sign where your current vibrational energy is at. Now when you learn to neutralize those thoughts (Neutrality 250 Hz, refer to the chart) by becoming aware of them, you move to the Middle level of Consciousness. The middle level of consciousness is about understanding how our beliefs create our reality. Thought like "I don't currently have this, then do I have", convert into "I have a belief that I'm not worthy of it and I believe that they have what I don't and I feel a resistance because of that".

When you question yourself that, you feel a certain kind of blockage before you could reach the answer to it. This is where you see the reason right there, where you become aware of the level of consciousness of reasoning (Reason 400 Hz). When we finally see the reason, the reason is that of the intellectual mind that says “okay, I can understand that my beliefs create my reality and when I change my beliefs, I change my reality.” So, beliefs create reality. This is a higher-level paradigm than the lower consciousness because the lower consciousness thinks that reality is fixed. It thinks that things are the way they are, that this is the way it is and I may or may not manifest anything different. But the Middle-level Consciousness realises that if we change our beliefs, we will experience a new reality, the intellect from within understands that, okay, this is something I can work on from within and then my outer reality will start changing as well.

You’ll see the bottom, shame, fear, guilt and the other negative emotions that really wants us to desire something, and then in order to reach the Middle Consciousness, you’ve to let go and observe from a neutral place, ‘Neutrality’, observe the thoughts you have, observe why you feel those emotions or why do you feel lack of something and then choosing to let them go and maybe completing your past a few times as well. However letting go is the doorway to the Middle Consciousness or the second paradigm. Now once you’re in the second paradigm, which is that of reasoning, understanding you start to move to the third paradigm.

The doorway to the Higher Consciousness is dropping all the intellectual ideas. It is understanding that, yes, beliefs create your reality but it is dropping the attachment to those beliefs, because different beliefs you have are different vehicles you use for a while but eventually you'll have to step out of the vehicle and get into a new one, or you're going to realise that you can just teleport places. That's when you start entering the Higher Consciousness. Because all beliefs are valid and most of the beliefs will eventually shift, you might have a belief that you can only make 40,000 a month but eventually, you'll let go of that belief to then make 80,000 a month. You'll have to let go of that belief and self-image you currently have in order to move to the next one into the third paradigm.

The higher consciousness is about understanding and going beyond the thoughts, the beliefs and into being in the present movement. We all are connected to the universe and that divide frequency can flow through any of us if we choose and the more we tune into it, the more we will experience it in our lives and the way we tune into it is by doing something we are passionate about. It is about connecting to our hearts and trusting the process. So just like Neutrality was the doorway to Middle Consciousness, similarly, the doorway to Higher Consciousness is about letting go, being in the moment and surrendering to the truth. It is about aligning with a higher level of energy, that is you, that is always around you can always pick up on but it's simply about you choosing it. And the more you choose it, by doing what you're passionate about. When I write my books or do research for them in the morning, it is my mind telling me, "this is what you're meant to do be doing", the more my ego gets out of the way, and I allow my higher self to come through, this high consciousness just flows through me.

The doorway to the middle consciousness is creating your own reality, understanding how your beliefs are a reflection of what you experience. And the doorway to the higher consciousness is moving from the head and into your heart, from having and doing into 'being', being who you truly are, being in the present moment and surrendering to the truth. And when you make that transition, your frequency will increase, you will then experience a reality that is equal to that change in vibration.

As we move up this chart, we'll see different personality traits, different versions of us that are in different states, different emotions. The reasoning and the intellect will get us so far but eventually there is a level higher than that. The lower levels of consciousness, shame, guilt, anger, those are on autopilot, thinking on a loop, "I'm not worthy", "I'm not that person", "I want this but don't have it", "how does he have what I want". Observe wherever you are, observe that state and you observe you move to the middle consciousness, to Neutrality.

Reality is a reflection, we always get a mirror reflection of what we believe to be true. At Lower Consciousness, we go change the mirror without changing our expressions first. At Middle Consciousness, we change our expressions to see the change reflected in the mirror, to change the reality we want to experiment. And at Higher Consciousness, we let go of the mirror altogether. It is about being in the present and letting go of the previous attachments.

If you are reading this book, then you're in vibrational resonance with moving up these levels because if you understand and perceive the higher level of consciousness it is possible you're already experiencing it or want to reach there. Look out for the doorways into each level of consciousness. That is the key to staying in higher vibrations. Be aware of the emotions to be aware of your vibrations.

Like I had mentioned before, don't think of lower, middle and higher consciousness as good or bad. If you're sad or feeling grief, then allow yourself to feel through it. It's good letting it out and experiencing a lower consciousness temporarily than remaining stuck in that state for too long. Always aiming to be happy and not accepting your authentic emotions might lead to another set of problems known as toxic positivity.

—

"The world isn't "good vibes only". It's just vibes, good or bad. Rejecting either good or bad vibes means rejecting fifty percent of the reality."

CHAPTER FIVE

Toxic Positivity

Toxic positivity is the belief that people should keep a positive mindset despite how severe or complex the situation is.

We all know those people who are always happy, shiny and utterly optimistic about everything. They're equipped with a clear-cut, exclusively positive approach to life, no matter how big or small. You'll probably notice when you talk to them about a specific situation you're dealing with, they'll sprinkle you with sweet optimism which is supposed to make your problems go away in an instant.

"You're going through a heartbreak? You'll get over it!"
"You got rejected for the job? Be positive!"
"You've been cheated on so many times that you've problems now trusting people? Don't be so negative!"

Statements like these come from a sincere place of love but also blissful ignorance. The problem is that these statements phrases contain a certain degree of denial of an indisputable part of life: suffering.

Toxic positivity is the refusal to see the negative, while solely focusing on the positive. Instead of facing reality as is it, it chooses rather a "fake-it-till-you-make-it" attitude, artificial smiles, and brushing anything undesirable under the carpet.

We can position ourselves towards these emotions by saying, "just be happy" or "stop being so negative!" The tricky part of such a position is that a positive mind state and the experience of happiness is indeed more preferable, but by rejecting and disapproving of grief, sadness, anger, our current mindstate will only get worse. What's even worse is the "good vibes only" kind of people that have zero tolerance for anything that they perceive as negative, insisting that they only surround themselves with happy, shiny and upbeat people. I'm not saying that they should surround themselves with utterly cynical or destructive people, but it's naive to expect that human beings are perpetually happy on command.

The world isn't "good vibes only". It's just vibes, good or bad. Rejecting either good or bad vibes means rejecting fifty percent of the reality.

Basically, everyone- even the most positive person you'll meet has a dark side. Toxic positivity is a recipe for creating a thick, sense shadow, that harbours all the underside traits that you're not supposed to have. Because you must wear the mask of happiness all the time, all your sadness and grief and other emotions that you can't show because you're forced to be positive are kicked down into the unconscious mind, rotting and creating a monster that will come to the surface when you least expect it.

Toxic positivity is an attempt to force positivity by rejecting any form of undesirable aspects of certain events, while true positivity is adopting a positive attitude towards these events while accepting the negative aspects at the same time. It's the middle way of being positive while leaving room for negative emotions as well and fully accepting that we're sad, grieving or feeling down.

Instead of saying "you'll get over it", we can say, "I understand it's a difficult situation. But you've coped in the past and I know you can cope with it again. Let me know if you need anything." So, by replacing toxic positivity with true positivity, we leave room for people to feel what they feel. I mean, how can we help people when we're denying them at the same time?

People that force you to be happy and positive, to simply stop grieving, that only want to associate with you when you radiate "good vibes", aren't a positive influence at all. They project their own unwillingness to face their negative emotions upon other people, forcing their mask on you that's similar to their own. By doing so, they sell themselves short on life, because they deny themselves and others the complete spectrum of what it means to be a human.

After experiencing some sort of loss, people inform you to "get over it". While people make such statements simply because they think it's comforting, it's also an easy method of avoiding somebody else's discomfort. Once you express frustration or sadness, someday informs you that 'happiness is a choice'. This implies that if you're experiencing negative emotions, then it is your choice, along with your own choice for not choosing to be happy. Such statements are generally well-intentioned, people simply do not know what else to say or how to be more empathetic.

Toxic positivity denies people from being their authentic selves, it can be harmful to someone who is having a hard time. Individuals find their emotions dismissed, ignored or outright invalidated. Toxic positivity informs the individual that the negative thoughts they're experiencing are wrong. It causes guilt. It delivers a message that if you're not finding a method to feel positive, even in the face of tragedy, then when doing something wrong. It prevents the individual to feel authentic emotions. We then turn these ideas on ourselves, internalising these toxic traits. Whenever we feel complicated or negative thoughts we then discredit, dismiss and reject these negative feelings. It stops development. It allows us to avoid experiencing things that could be painful but also. It denies us the capacity to face challenging feelings that may eventually cause development and much more profound understanding.

The Dark Side of Optimism:

Suppressed emotions: If you redirect your thoughts towards something positive, notice if you're actually simply suppressing your negative emotions instead. Suppressing your emotions is like getting a piece of bread and chucking it to the back of the cupboard. Over time, that will rot, mold and going to get worse and worse. There was a scientific study where they got two groups of people are weren't much invested in horror movies to watch those movies.

The first group was told to watch it as normal and their emotions were calculated in the end. The second group was asked to watch it but not show any kind of emotions as they watched it. The second group ended up feeling far stronger than the first group because they were asked to suppress their emotions.

For most things, endless positivity isn't beneficial. It's better to focus on the negative for a while, understand that emotion and when you do that, it will get dispelled, that negative emotion won't have that power over you anymore once you acknowledge it, let yourself feel through it and let it go in a healthy manner. If we don't do this and suppress our emotions, we don't live authentically. It's like we're living with a mask on the front of us, we're not really being ourselves, we're not showing the world who we actually are and it can cause a lot of disconnects. It can cause internal problems. As Carl Jung says, "everyone has a shadow". Everybody has a dark side. And instead of suppressing and pushing away that dark side, we have to learn to accept it.

Emotions are cognitively assembled conscious feelings, which means our emotions are actually a conscious construction of our mind.

True positivity is focusing on the good in life and being grateful while toxic positivity is ignoring the bad in life and suppressing your emotions.

The repercussion of a repressed identity:

Now, imagine it's a cold day and you wake up in the morning, you walk outside with a jacket on your way to work and you go get yourself a lovely cup of tea before you reach there. You grab the cup and it warms up your hand, you take a sip and it takes away the wintery chill. How do you feel? Pretty positive, happy and cozy, right? But for an individuals with repressed emotions, they will certainly not feel anything about it.

When the individual turned off the tap between negative events and negative emotions, they also turned off the tap between positive events and positive emotions. The individual almost doesn't feel anything. And this is definitely not good, we all want to feel positive emotions, right? Not only that but you use your emotions, negative or positive to guide you to live a better life. If you're thinking of quitting a job and you feel scared it's probably because you don't know what other options you have and you're feeling a bit lost. When you're scared of losing a friend, it's probably because you value that friend. We can use emotions as pieces of information or as data to piece together the kind of life we want to live. If you shut off your emotions, you lose that capability as well. If you shut off your emotions to stop feeling the negative emotions, then you can't feel the positive emotions either.

To be a "positive vibes only" kind of person, whilst it seems great in reality, it can cause a lot of grief. At the end of the day, there is no particular piece of advice that rings true for everybody. Personal context matters a lot when you apply this in your life. The world isn't all sunshine and rainbows but it's also not all grey clouds and rain. Being positive is great, it can greatly impact your life, but be careful of the nuisances that can unfold while going into the real world.

Emotional Baggage:

Emotional Baggage is the feelings you have about your past and the things that have happened to you, which often have a negative effect on your behaviour and attitudes. It's having emotions and feelings from the past that are somehow still influencing you and limiting our experience in life. We felt it 7 years ago but they're still impacting us even now.

It generally takes place if the other person has betrayed you or left you and instead of dealing with the situation then and there, you just act like nothing has happened and it doesn't affect you. But here's the thing, it did affect you. And now you're left wondering why you can't look at people, friendships or relationships the same way.

Now, if you had treated that previous situation differently with the person who betrayed you or left you, if you had acknowledged it and mourned that event, you may find it a lot easier with the next similar situation you're in.

But because you ignored that previous event, a peculiar transaction took place and with that a new rule was created with how you were going to treat yourself, that you're willing to accept that previous behaviour from the last person who betrayed you or left you, as something just happens to me. It's your own subconscious mind's way of dealing with it and minimising the pain from it by not acknowledging the pain of betrayal from that person.

Our subconscious mind has 2 directives, the pursuit of pleasure and avoidance of pain. Now the event when the previous person betrayed or left you without closure or explanation and the new rule that you've created with it which is 'this is okay, this is something I'll willing to put up with, this just happens to me and I don't think I need to mourn about it to face any feelings of pain' are both calcified. They become hardened over time, so you can carry them around whenever you go conveniently. This is learnt behavioural patterns based on your denial of choosing to face your pain in the past which affects your day to day choices now.

Emotional Baggage can be viewed as something called the 'Trapped Emotions' which exist all over our bodies. A trapped emotion is simply a grouping of energy that holds the energy of lower consciousness emotions like sadness, grief or shame.

Setting up boundaries can help you with the emotional baggage. Setting boundaries is simply the way you're going to stick up for yourself the next time someone hurts you. Simply acknowledge that the next time something this messed up or unacceptable happens, that you won't ignore it and you will deal with that pain right there and now.

Another way of letting go of emotional baggage is to forgive yourself for carrying that baggage. Somewhere at some point, you blamed yourself for taking care of the situation poorly and not allowing yourself to heal completely. Forgiving yourself can be one of the easiest things to do because we're typically at the bottom of the list of the things to take care of. So, do yourself a favour, forgive yourself for not checking in on yourself and just remember to say, "Hey, how're you doing", once in a while. Even that momentary level of awareness can be life-changing. And when you can forgive yourself, it becomes insurmountably easier to forgive others and let those old grudges go that you've been carrying around.

Your emotional baggage is a construct of your mind. It represents the unnecessary suffering we bring upon ourselves when we feel responsible for a negative outcome. So, the real trick in dealing with it is first acknowledging it then taking responsibility for any different choices you would like to make for the future, then finally dropping the bag forever.

—

"It's not what happens to you, but how you react to it that matters."

\- Epictetus

CHAPTER SIX

WHY DO YOU ATTRACT THE WRONG PEOPLE

Wherever you go in life, there will always be toxic people in your life. And it's easy to feel frustrated, especially when they take up all your emotional energy. When you feel annoyed by the toxicity in your life, it's tempting to blame others and ask the world, "why me?". Well, you should into that question yourself, how your thoughts, feelings and behavioural patterns attract toxic people. The types of people you attract have a lot to do with who you are. Now, I'm not saying that you're doing something wrong, but you may want to examine that it is about you that is so alluring to the toxic personalities.

If you feel like you're a magnet to the wrong people then in this chapter we're going to have a little overview as to why it seems like that.

Being easygoing is a great trait and it attracts people whether they're toxic or not. An easy-going person has a knack for putting others at ease in an uncomfortable situation. If that sounds like you, then others might describe you as a patient person or a peacemaker. Although your relaxed personality is not at fault, your mellow nature makes you a target for toxic people. They interpret your carefree attitude as a weakness and assume that you're easy to control. And once they're set their eyes on you, it's easy for them to manipulate you and you wind up doing things that you would rather not do. To prevent this, cultivate an awareness of other people's intentions and avoid the tendency to commit to requests automatically.

Most people work towards becoming better listeners, but good listeners often attract troubled people. You might find yourself stuck in one-sided conversations as someone keeps emotionally dumping on you with complete disregard for your time. If you're an empathetic listener, then the toxic person won't hesitate to share their negative energy with you. They might talk for hours and not once ask for your input. That's narcissistic behaviour and in other to avoid them, decide how much time you want to spend with them before meeting them.

Some people are fixers, they solve problems, repair broken things and even try to fix people. Although this can be positive and even altruistic, it makes you a target for toxic people. If you're compassionate and help others without asking anything in return, toxic individuals see this as an opportunity. And if you have a hard time leaving things be, you might be having a hard time in your relationships. The solution is to let things go. Not everything that seems broken needs fixing, at least not by you. When you understand this and stay away from toxic people, it becomes easier to protect yourself in a healthy way.

Generosity is a positive characteristic, and you shouldn't feel bad about being a giving person. Whether you offer up your time, talent or resources to other people, you become a good role model for others and you might attract a few toxic people too, especially if you give freely without being mindful of your boundaries. Toxic people flock to generosity like a moth to a flame. They know you'll give them the attention and emotional energy that they desire and you might even cater to their needs at your own expense. The bad news is, the more you give in, the more they'll demand. You give them an inch and they'll take a mile. To avoid being stuffed full of resentment and bitterness for toxic people, establish and reinforce your boundaries by saying 'No' more often.

People who are passionate and energetic tend to attract toxic people. That's because toxic individuals want to drag you down. Toxic people often give up on their dreams out of fear. When they see you living life in a way that they desire and believe is impossible, they seek the satisfaction and validation of watching you fail. If you open up about your ideas and goals, they'll discourage you and break you down. Toxic people see successful and driven people as materialistic, selfish and unrealistic. And they won't hesitate to criticize you for it. To avoid toxic people who want nothing more than sinking your ship, be intentional with whom your surround yourself with. Choose to spend time with people who are like you: passionate, reserved, motivated and genuinely positive. And moving forward, protect yourself from toxicity by not opening up to pessimistic or close-minded people.

Most people can agree that humans are generally good but there's always going to be a bad apple in the bunch. Some people, however, refuse to accept the dark realities of human nature. They believe that the bad apple can always be made good again, even when things are hopeless. If you don't accept things like deception, greed and possessiveness for what they are, you most likely hold on to unhealthy and toxic friendships and relationships hoping for change and chances are you brush off red flags like it's nothing and continue to spend time with them. If that sounds like you, your tolerance for toxicity is high. You've likely had a lot of experience enduring toxic or abusive behaviours, maybe because you didn't probably realise what was happening. Your positivity can put you at risk because it often brushes negative emotions like anxiety and anger under the rug. Don't wait until the situation becomes unbearable. Instead, harness the power of your intuition, it could help you predict danger. Remain optimistic but be realistic about people too.

Everyone has a past and we all have emotional baggage that we carry from it, whether that comes from your childhood, past relationships or friendships, or challenging experiences, emotional baggage can make you feel insecure and often make you think you don't deserve certain things you want. Toxic people love vulnerabilities. They're using your insecurities against you. Don't let a toxic person use you. Instead, work through your issues by yourself, or by someone you trust. Move through your life with security and strength because only you can protect yourself from toxic people. You might have noticed that the traits that attract toxic people tend to be positive. But you shouldn't discard these characteristics. They make you who you are. What you should do, is to be aware and be realistic. There are always going to be toxic people out there and you'll run into them. When that happens, be ready. Protect yourself and while you're at it, set an example for the people in your life. Your positivity can transform negative energy, helping those who mean well and want to improve themselves.

—

"Everything that irritates us about others can lead us to an understanding of ourselves."

- Carl Jung

CHAPTER SEVEN

WALLS OF DEFENSE

Do you get annoyed or upset when people ask how you're feeling? Are you quick to brush off any concerns that people may have about you because you don't think it's any of their business? Maybe you're not comfortable opening up to others or just like getting overly sentimental. It may be a sign you're emotionally repressed and that you've created a wall of defense to disassociate you from reality, people or feeling anything. You constantly avoid all conversations about your feelings.

Other signs that you have a wall set up unconsciously to protect you from feeling things include: you have problems finding a friend to confide in or have trouble making a meaningful relationship or friendship. This may be because you struggle with emotional intimacy. Since it forces to you open up, be vulnerable and confront your true feelings while sharing about your life, you may end up running away or get defensive and struggle to emotionally connect with them.

Another sign could be you're 'just fine'. Every time someone asks you how you are, you may reassure your friends and family that you're great, in a way that it seems as if, if you can convince them you're fine, you convince yourself you're fine as well. You tell them everything is well when you don't mean any of it. You're not comfortable admitting when you're not okay or to let people see you struggle. Instead of asking for help or to confront your feelings, you just repress your emotions and bottle them up inside your wall of defense to protect yourself but as we all know it does more harm than good.

One other sign could be you rarely get emotional. Do people describe you as withdrawn, different or detached? You don't cry, or get upset. Neither do you get excited about anything? Not only do you dislike talking about your feelings but you would rather show everyone that you don't have any at all. You may have been badly hurt in the past and you don't want to feel overwhelmed by your emotions again, so you just resolve to close yourself off and not feel anything at all. This led you to create a wall of defense for yourself.

Lashing out and emotional volatility are clear signs that you're repressing your very strong emotions. Instead of resolving them in a healthy way, you may be pushing them down as if they're not there but your emotions will come out in a much more problematic manner where you take all your negativity out on yourself or those around you.

If you avoid your loved ones when they're mad at you or agree to do things that you don't want to do to make other people happy, it could be a sign you've set a wall of defense.

Denial is a very common defense mechanism, since it may feel like it's much easier to pretend that your problems don't exist than to find a solution. This difficulty admitting to yourself when something is wrong could be a sign of an emotional wall you've for yourself.

Another sign related to that could be, you hold grudges against people and you have problems letting feelers of anger and disappointment go. Harbouring grudges against people and being vindictive is a very telling sign that you're holding back on your emotions. You may be having a hard time forgiving others because you can't come in term with all the pain that they have caused you, even if it was unintentional. But holding on to grudges only shows that you're not prepared to deal with your emotions and you would rather let them linger over time.

—

*"He who knows, does not speak.
He who speaks, does not talk."*

-Lao Tzu

CHAPTER EIGHT

INTROVERSION

Since over 60% of the book readers are introverts, according to a study, I want to highlight some points for the introverts out there and how their perspective, strengths and the ability to introspect helps to know themselves better, how by taking time away from people and spending time with their own self helps them to understand their emotions, idealisations and passions better. So, let's take a moment to overview introverts or introversion in general.

By many, being introverted is seen as a weakness. Introverts rather stay in the background often hesitate to make a decision and get fatigued by social interaction. But these so-called weaknesses are easily compensated by a series of strengths that are generally overlooked, despite the fact that they are invaluable in many different settings. The fact is: we live in an extroverted world, in which extroverted qualities are desirable over introverted qualities.

Introverts often spend a good portion of their time in solitude, during which they think deeply about life. An introvert's brain works differently than an extrovert's brain, which makes an introvert process information more deeply. A strong aspect of thinking is the ability to reflect on life and explore different future scenarios. Although this could lead to worrying and rumination, it is an opportunity to design a life that suits them, and builts strategies to accomplish them. Introverts are not only deep thinkers, they are often good writers too. The practice of journaling is a powerful tool to reflect on the past and makes sense out of it, in order to design a better future. An introverted mind is great at planning out life step by step, because it carefully imagines pitfalls and possibilities, and is aware of the things that many extroverts overlook.

People often say being around people energizes the extrovert, but exhausts the introvert. And from my own experience, it is very true. After a period of socialization, we need time alone to recover and replenish our energy. This means that we are most energized when we're alone, and thus, the most productive. When you're the most productive in solitude, you are gifted with an opportunity for great, creative accomplishments. This could be something artistic, or perhaps creating an application or even writing a book. These things are not made during meetings, not on networking events, they are made by the creative individual and executed in solitude.

A coping mechanism of not wanting to be in the center of attention is finding ways to express ourselves. That's why many introverts become good at artistic traits. When I was small, I used to express myself by doodles and writing short snippets. Today, I express myself by writing books and doing podcasts. And these are a way for me to express myself than giving a speech to a crowd. So, an introvert's creativity is partly born out of the avoidance of small talk and being around people all the time.

Introverts are great observers. While the extroverted people are busy shouting at each other, an introvert remains in the background and simply watches. They closely register what is said and only speak when there is something useful to say. As Lao Tzu said, "He who knows, does not speak. He who speaks, does not know." Lao Tzu simply points to the idea that when you speak, you cut yourself off from, possibly, valuable information that the environment gives you. That's why we see many extroverts talk on and on when they don't know what's happening, just for the rewarding act of getting their voice heard. Introverts, however, do know what's going on because they've seen it. This gives them a position of power because they know what others don't know.

Introverts tend to be great observers and often over analyze things in solitude, they've trained themselves to pay attention to details that extroverted people overlook because they're too busy chatting with each other. Some people may perceive this characteristic as a bit annoying, but I think it is an invaluable trait. How can mankind reach greatness if there aren't people who pay attention to the small stuff? As they say: the devil is in the details. It is necessary to have people with the ability to look at things from different perspectives, explore different scenarios and highlight weaknesses. Without the observant eye of an introvert, an ambitious project might go to waste in the blink of an eye.

Introverts are great listeners. Listening is a vital component of a healthy relationship with another person. Because they are good listeners they process and internalise a lot of information about the other person so, they get a deeper understanding of them. This way, introverts can empathize with others more easily, because they know what they're going through. Especially because they have the ability to think deeply and imaginative another person's suffrage for themselves. The way introverts handle their loved ones leads to deep and long-lasting bonds.

Highly introverted people that loved being alone, are unlikely to be codependent. Codependent people cannot live without a partner and cannot imagine spending the Saturday evenings alone. According to the stoics not needing external things to live a happy life is strength. Because, at the end of the day, other people are beyond your control. In our society, we are always dependent, in some way, on other people. But the simple fact that you find contentment in being by yourself exerts power: it prevents others from people abusing the need for companionship that many people have. Companionship can be a great addition to your life but because you don't need that, you are not enslaved by it.

Introverts don't like small talk. The whole "how are you", "can you believe this weather", "did you see the game last night", chitchats are worthless. Due to their disdain for idle chatter, they're seen by most as unsociable and that is not the case. Introverts want to get straight down to the deepest of things. They want to hear your deepest thoughts, your desires and dreams and none of that "I'm fine, how are you?" talk. Introverts know that you have a story to tell and they want to hear it. They want to know your opinions and questions and answers to the questions that are infrequently spoken about because of their deep topics. Introverts have a therapist, guidance, counselor mentality and charisma causing us to make you feel more comfortable while speaking your mind and soul. This is good for everyone around. Introverts give the satisfaction of having a meaningful conversation with someone without having to fill the empty space with chit-chat.

Introverts are good leaders. A recent poll shows that not all successful leaders are extroverts. Outgoing individuals use their charisma and spunk to command attention and get things done while reserved bosses lay low and observe their underlinings and always know what's the best for them, the person and the situation. They never speak just to be heard or because they're the boss. They speak to assist and help others because introverts imagine themselves in quite every situation just to be prepared. They're careful and attentive, humble and prepared and they're comfortable working alone, showing that good leadership isn't always flashy.

We all know the quiet person have the loudest minds. Introverts spend a lot of time in their own heads. From this, they know themselves pretty well. Aside from being silent critics, introverts are constantly having inner monologues, evaluating themselves and their choices in everyday situations. Thus they may rarely have an existential crisis and they can figure out their strengths and weaknesses. They know who they are, what they want and what is important to them. They might not just tell you all of that information. You can just say that they're silent but they're confident.

Introverts don't speak quite often, so when they do, every single word is carefully chosen ahead of time. Sometimes due to this, introverts may take a while to get a sentence out, since they're mentally preparing and rehearsing each word before they say it. Since introverts take a while to express themselves, many extroverts just ignore them and talk over them. This can cause introverts to become even more shy so that they don't get ignored again, as this is embarrassing. So, if an introverted friend speaks up, pay close attention, because what they have to say is probably important.

—

"Dream as big as you like. You are serving no one by dreaming small."

CHAPTER NINE

WHY THE WORLD OF IMAGINATION IS IMPORTANT

What is imagination to you? Most of us are told that imagination is separate from reality but this is only in the initial stages. What if you knew that anything you could see on the screen of your mind could also be yours in reality? You would start appreciating imagination in a completely different way. How much time do you spend daydreaming, fantasizing or getting lost in your imagination? Probably not nearly as much as you should. Most of us are taught to do the opposite from a young age, to snap out of our imagination and come back to reality not realising that this reality is filled with physical manifestations that were once conceived in someone's mind.

From the phone you have in your hand to the movie you watched yesterday, these were all once nothing more than a thought in someone's head. Of course, there is a difference between creative imagination and endless daydreaming that inevitably disrupts your actual life but with an appreciation for the true power of your imagination and the willpower to chase your visions, you can ultimately have anything you want. Imagination, like most things, is a muscle. The more you use it, the better you get at it. So many of us stop getting lost in our imagination as we used to when we grow up and leave our vivid daydreams behind with our childhood. If you were taught from a young age that anything you can see in your mind can yours in reality with the right actions, you would most likely keep practising it into adulthood.

Einstein once said that Imagination is more powerful than Knowledge. Without imagination, nothing worthwhile will ever be created. Pretty much all great leaders and successful people have set aside time to use their imagination to project new ideas and future outcomes. But only that but it is incredibly nourishing for your inner child. Positive thoughts have a massively healthy effect on your body and can begin the course of a new direction in your life. Set some time apart to get in touch with your imagination and inner child, to get a new perspective in your life or even just something to entertain you, your imagination can do it by itself if you allow it and before you know it, you have tons of new ideas.

Life isn't that different from the fairy tales we're told about as kids. Life is what you make it. I know plenty of people who have gotten what they want from life and led amazing existences. Take time to imagine what the perfect life would look like, don't hold back, really visualise an amazing future for yourself, from the amount of money in your pocket to your dream job. Dream as big as you like. You are serving no one by dreaming small. Life is meant to be filled with joy and abundance. Keep constructing the ideal future in your mind. Over time, your dream vision will become clearer and clearer. The more you visualise, the more you'll start to attract the people and opportunities that will lead you to your destination. This is known as the law of attraction. You can use your imagination to attract whatever you like.

There are other ways how practising imagination that lead you towards positive changes in your life. For example, the self-image you have of yourself is the person you are. If you visualise a new self-image, the person you want to be, with consistency, that will be the person you will become, when combined with persistent action. If you're feeling nervous about a future event or outcome, you can take time to visualise it going really well, giving yourself the affirmation that you need about this. If you're feeling unwell or you're in pain, you can visualise about being healthy again or visualise about the things you can do that you love when you're well again. Open your mind to the power of your thoughts and start experimenting with yourself. So the belief in your imagination and affirmations can amplify.

Each thought contains its own energetic frequency and becomes stronger and stronger with every locus. Be mindful and start using your thoughts carefully. Your belief in this practise will have a massively positive effect on your ability to create whatever you like. You'll be astonished at how conscious thoughts can change your life. Keep believing and dreaming.

—

"Most people don't really want freedom, because freedom involves responsibility. And most people are frightened of responsibility."

- Sigmund Freud

CHAPTER TEN

LOCUS OF CONTROL

A locus is simply a point, place or location where something occurs. A person's Locus of Control could be internal or external. People who base their success on their own work and believe they control their life have an internal locus of control. However, people who attribute their success or failure to outside influences have an external locus of control.

For example, let's say you're a person of internal locus of control and you get a promotion at work or achieve any other type of success, you'll probably attribute that positive end result to the work you've put in, in other words, your success was a direct result of your hard work. If on the other hand, you have an external locus of control, then you might attribute that promotion or success to external or environmental factors like luck, fate, timing, some people and such.

Let's say you're denied a promotion. If your locus of control is internal, you would find a way to blame yourself for the perceived failure. If your locus of control is external, it would be easy, even natural, to blame outside sources beyond your control like, "my boss doesn't like me" or "it was too hard for me anyway".

Individuals who have an internal locus of control identity with more responsibility whether those actions or the end results are good or bad. They do not accept outside influence for the outcome, no matter what that is. If this person did not get back to work before lunch, they would think that they should've eaten in the office. The results of their actions are theirs and theirs alone to bear.

On the other hand, the person who identities with an external locus of control looks at everything around as a part of success or failure. In many ways, they believe in the team aspect more than those who use internal locus of control as they will always praise those around them for a job well done even if they didn't have anything to do with it at all.

They're drawbacks to both though. An internally focused person would be hard on themselves and constantly analyse what they did wrong. That perspective almost forces these individuals to be hard-charging individuals that at a time can assure a take-no-prisoners attitude. Conversely, those who have an external focus may come off as someone who just doesn't accept responsibilities, while they can be team players if the result is not a positive one, they'll be the first one to complain that something outside their personal control attributed to the shortfall.

External locus of control is a mindset that most people

have. If something goes wrong, they're quick to point fingers at someone else. People with this mindset say things like, "It's not my fault", "There's nothing I could have done". They're full of excuses and tend to shift the responsibility on other people.

Some people adopt this mindset because they believe that they would seem more competent if they blame other people for a negative outcome. After all, it stops them from looking bad. Other people use this excuse because it gives them an excuse to look bad or to be lazy, saying things like, "my coach is terrible, that's why I couldn't do it". The consequences of this mindset are that you give up all responsibility and in doing so allow other people to control large aspects if not your entire life. This is a disempowering mindset, and although it is much easier but it doesn't help you. By choosing this mindset you're robbing yourself of the freedom you get from having full control over your life. Now bear in mind, when I say control, I don't exactly mean controlling those actions or thoughts, rather the acceptance of them and having sense a control that allows to experience that it's up to you and how you want to change or perceive them.

People with an internal locus of control take responsibility for all the things in their life, both good and bad. They believe everything in their life is a result of the decisions they've made. In bad situations, they take full responsibility for their actions, they knew it turned out bad because of something they chose to do. To most people, this sounds completely unhealthy, to keep blaming yourself. However, the aim of having an internal locus of control is not to make you feel bad or make change because you feel guilty. Their aim is to show just how much power you have over your life and how you create all aspects of your life.

Let's take one last example of Tim. Tim always thinks about how he has no partner, how he hates his job and earns very little money. Tim doesn't have any passion for life. He has an external locus of control, so he chooses to blame outside sources for the way his life is. He says the reason he doesn't have a partner is because women aren't attracted to him and that's because he was born unattractive. Tim says the reason he says a bad job is because when he was at school, the teacher wasn't good enough and he didn't receive a proper education limited his potential ever since. Tim also says his boss is ignorant and never notices the work Tim does. If the boss was to ever pay attention to Tim and the way he was doing, he would definitely give him a raise. That's why Tim doesn't earn much, he is waiting for his boss to finally notice him. He mostly thinks, "How am I supposed to feel passionate when no one gives me a chance?", because he has an external locus of control. He's waiting for other people to help him out.

One day Tim decides to adapt his locus of control to internal. Here's what happens: he takes full responsibility for his life. He thinks about the things he really wants and is important to him and suddenly his mindset changes: no partner, bad job and low salary becomes is because of Tim's own action. This makes Tim feel terrible. He has created his terrible life for himself. But then he a simple thought, if I have the power to create all these negative actions in my life, I also have the power to create positive things. I'm at the center of this all, so if I decide to make a change then everything will change.

Suddenly, Tim has a huge sense of power and control over his life. This is exactly what the internal locus of control does. Knowing that he now has a great sense of control of life, he looks at the different areas of his life that he really wants a change in and starts working on it. He thinks why he has no partner. He came to the conclusion that he put very little effort into his appearance, granted he isn't the best looking guy but he's also never put any effort into making himself presentable. He stopped looking down on himself and thinks about how he can change this. He searches for YouTube videos about which appearance fits you, asks his friends about choosing the right outfit, and makes an effort in looking presentable and different.

Tim also realises that he's unattractive not because of his physical appearance but because he is so negative when he's around women. Even before they speak, he's thinking negative things about himself and the whole situation. So, he decides to stop this immediately too.

Tim thinks of how he created a situation of not liking his job for a lot of years but did nothing about it. With his new sense of power, he starts looking at new jobs that he really likes, he searches for a few jobs and finds a few he would be passionate about. When Tim got the interview for the new job, he had a lot more confidence in the past, because, unlike the last job, this one didn't like he was being rushed into a decision or he was simply following the herd. It was his own decision. His positive attitude made him right for the next job. Tim got promoted really soon in his next job since he was passionate about it and hence started making more money as well. Tim knew the amount of money he was earning was because of him because he decided to work on himself.

Tim continued his self-improvement in working on himself. Due to this people, started finding him attractive and filled with good vibes because he simply was in control of his life, actions and goals.

It sounds like a fairy tale but it really does. Back in 2019, when I was really low, sort of life Tim in the above example. I didn't know anything about self-improvement and I simply wasn't thinking about the locus of control. But a simple thought popped into my head, if I'm responsible for all the terrible stuff I've created for myself then I'm also capable of creating great things. And surely that year I tried something new, I wrote my first book that year.

You have to think that you're the co-creator of your life and think of something that you don't usually do and then that happens in your life. For example, I always wanted to have my own podcast, so in 2021, I went ahead and before I knew it, I was recording my first episode and releasing it on Spotify, google podcast and iTunes. So, this wasn't a normal activity for me and thus, showed me how much influence I have over my reality. It was really simple but while I was recording the podcast, I knew I could create anything I wanted because all I had to do was create different decisions. It's fun and rewarding to know how much control you've over your life, actions and reality.

—

"Between stimulus and response, there is a space.
In that space is our power to choose our response.
In our response lies our growth and our freedom."

\- Victor E. Frankl

CHAPTER ELEVEN

Internal Monologue

What is an internal monologue? Simply put, the voice in which you're reading this sentence right now is your internal monologue.

So, in your head, I want you to yell the sentence, "I like crickets!". Just in your head. Don't say it out loud. And now we're going to do the same thing but this time instead of yelling, I want you to whisper, "I like crickets."

Now, was the actual volume of your inner voice actually different when you yelled verses when you whispered it? Your inner voice can feel like you're hearing yourself think, but it lives in a completely different part of your brain. So, when you're just going about your day and doing things, do you think in words and complete sentences? I do, but a lot of people don't. Unless they're reading or writing, a lot of people were reported thinking in pictures, actions or images, rather than words and sentences.

According to scientists, there are three major types of

thinkers. There are verbal thinkers, who think in whole words and sentences. Pattern thinkers think in patterns and connections, which may also feel like thinking in actions and emotions. Then there are visual thinkers who think in terms of pictures, images and scenarios. Most people probably do a little bit of all three. But it also means that not everyone has an internal monologue.

One study looked at how similar reading dialogues are to hearing them. They had participants read different sentences in their heads. These are the two kinds of sentences they were asked to read in their head.

The man said, “I like crickets”.
The man said that he like crickets.

The first one includes a dialogue. The second sentence means the same thing, however, it doesn’t have a dialogue. The study found that when the sentences contain dialogue, parts of the auditory cortex are activated. You’re actually hearing what the characters have to say while reading it in your head. Even when you’re just replaying or imagining a conversation in your head. This is different from being a verbal thinker. An inner monologue doesn’t activate the auditory cortex but an inner dialogue does.

And it turns out, what your inner reading voice sounds like is not universal. Some people read in their heads all in one voice: their own. I also fall in the same category. But other people read in a different voice, with an identifiable gender, pitch or tone that is different from their own voice. The other voice may be consistent when reading or it may change based on what you’re reading. Some people even read in multiple voices and some people don’t hear a voice while reading at all.

So, without being able to see or hear what’s going on in someone else’s mind, we tend to assume that our experiences are universal and because of that a lot of research about this wasn’t done until recently. We’re just starting to learn more about the variations in how our mind works, and how we experience the world a little differently.

Professor Russel Hurlburt conducted research on this

about 40 years ago. Hurlburt created a device that the participants would wear and when the device would beep, they had to write their thoughts down that they were having in that precise moment. And they would try their best to write down clearly what was going in their head. His research showed that many of the participants couldn't clearly describe what their thoughts were. According to his research, he concluded that there are five types of thinking or voices that we hear in our head: Inner monologue, inner seeing/imagery, feelings, unsymbolized thinking and sensory awareness.

Inner monologue is hearing yourself or someone else's voice inside your head or recalling a number or conversation audibly in your head. Inner seeing is a visual representation of your thoughts, almost like a photo of a place you've visited in the past.

Feeling is a conscious awareness of an emotional process such as feeling sad after a loved one has passed away. Unsymbolized thinking is where there is nothing particularly going in your head, like pouring a cup of coffee in your head and without telling yourself what you've to do there, you just do it by yourself subconsciously.

Sensory awareness is a fun one. It's paying attention to a sensory aspect for an unimportant aspect such as you're listening to me talking but maybe you caught that glass reflection on my spectacles and that's what you're focused on instead of hearing me speak.

All of these are happening all the time, constantly hearing your own voice, even somebody else's texts, I can hear it while I'm reading it. For example, while reading a text if it has a break to the next line, I'll actively pause my inner monologue until I've reached the next line and continue reading it in my head. But not everyone has an inner voice or inner imagery. Some people can't visualise things or pictures in their heads (known as Aphantasia).

Most of us were taught to 'think before you speak', but the people who don't have an inner monologue can't really do that. People without inner monologue have said that when they're watching movies and there is a voice-over of the character's thoughts, that was just for TV, that it's not real. And for many of us like me, it's non-stop. Spot the people who speak their minds, these may be the people who might not have an inner voice because they're just saying as they're thinking. And I particularly want to focus on people who have an inner voice like me, that always kind of seem like they're stuck, daydreaming, looking at something distractedly or maybe they didn't hear what people are saying because they wondered off on their trail of thoughts following their inner voice. I want to focus on the importance of having an inner voice or monologue.

Have you ever been talking to yourself in your head when a friend walks in? Well, everyone talks to themselves, whether it's out loud or in their head. When I'm on super-long road trips, I tend to have a conversation with myself. People while hearing internal monologue not only are having silent conversations with themselves, but it often feels like we can hear our conversations out loud even though it's happening in our heads.

The Soviet psychologist Lev Vygotsky believed that our inner voice occurred because of the internalization of the external speech. For when you hear yourself or another person speak out loud, you internalise the sound of it and recreate the sound you've perceived in your mind. That's why your inner voice might sound like your voice and when you're thinking about friends might say after you've met them after long, you've recreated that homely voice of them greeting you.

Scientists have found through neurological experiments that the same part of the brain when we talk out loud is used when we are using our internal monologue. This is called Broca's area named after the scientist who discovered the link between speech and this part of the brain. When we use Broca's area, simultaneously we are using the same muscles in our throat that we use just before we make sound come out of our mouths: the Larynx.

So, what's the importance of having internal monologue? Well, it is quite not known but here are some listed points that I think are true for their importance. It might be an evolutionary step as our inner voices help us with tasks. For example, chess players who have an inner voice are reported to perform better. Our inner voice can also act as a motivator for ourselves, often in difficult situations. Artists use it to discover the depth of their imagination while their inner voice guides them through their imaginary world before they express it to the whole world. Actors use their internal monologue to rehearse the lines and timings of their speech in their head to allocate a suitable outcome to the real-world stage delivery. More or else, it helps us experiment with our thoughts and create different scenarios before actually facing them in real life so as to choose the appropriate response in the real world, it also helps us to juggle through different perspectives. However, engaging too much with your internal monologue can be distracting or may lead to overthinking. So, be careful to look out for that.

—

"Be yourself and don't apologise."

CHAPTER TWELVE

The Pygmalion Effect

The Pygmalion effect is the phenomenon whereby higher expectations lead to higher performance. It can be best understood by a circle where our beliefs about another person's abilities influence our actions toward the other person. This action has an impact on others' beliefs about themselves. The beliefs about themselves cause the others actions toward us, which again reinforce our beliefs about that person. And so on and on and on.

Let's look at an example to understand this better. Imagine you are the coach of a basketball team and you observe your team on the first day: Chris and Joe are new members of your team. Chris reminds you of a famous player. Joe reminds you of an annoying boy from your high school years. Unconsciously you decide what to expect of each one of them. Your beliefs influence your actions: when Chris enters the court you are happy to see him. When he plays you push him to do better, practice harder, stay an extra hour. If he makes a mistake you explained to him how to improve.

When Joe comes in you hardly notice him. You're glad to see him score but you don't give him much feedback and don't invest extra time in his training. When Joe does a mistake you are a little annoyed. Your actions impact their beliefs about themselves: Chris feels you appreciate him and he appreciates you in return. He believes in his own success. Joe feels you have little patience and appreciation for him he does not believe in his own success. Their beliefs about themselves cause their actions toward you: Chris finds more and more joy and playing and he never misses a training session. During the games, he gives a hundred percent all the time. Whereas, Joe finds less joy in playing than before and doesn't give his full effort in the games. He starts to miss the training sessions sometimes, which reinforces your beliefs about them: you see how Chris enjoys playing, how he trains hard and shows a fast increase in his performance. Joe seems not to be very motivated, his skills don't increase as much and he starts to show up less. You knew it right away and think that your instincts were right, but however, this was all based on your beliefs about them.

The Pygmalion effect is also known as the Rosenthal experiment named after a research of Robert Rosenthal at Harvard. In a first study, he challenged test subjects to coach rats through a maze. Half the group was told their rats were extremely intelligent and specifically trained, the other half were told that their rats were dumb. In reality, the rats were all the same.

During the experiment however, the "smart" rats performed well better than the "dumb" ones. This showed how the expectations of the coaches influenced even the performance of rats. Rosenthal then did the Pygmalion effect in school study, at the beginning of the school year, a group of elementary school teachers were told that some of their new pupils had extraordinary talent and potential. This information which was completely made up was given about random average students in each class.

All students had done the IQ test in advance. By the end of the year, the students that were described as more talented had significantly increased their performance in the IQ tests compared to the rest of the class. Robert Rosenthal concluded: "When we expect certain behaviors of others we are likely to act in ways that make the expected behavior more likely to occur."

This is mostly a learnt behaviour and otherwise shows how having the belief and treating them as such would have a positive effect on the other person. This also symbolises the power of positive affirmations given to a person that their perspective of themselves changes with time and so, they perform much better.

—

"The quality of your writing will be directly related to your understanding of the human behaviour."

- Bong Joon Ho

CHAPTER THIRTEEN

THE DUALITY OF A HUMAN

We are taught right now that we living in a world of constant and increasing polarity. It's either black or white, or us vs them, right or wrong. There is no middle, there is no grey, just polarity. And as we all know, polarity is a state in which two ideas or opinions are completely opposite from each other. The problem with polarity and absolutes is that it eliminates the individuality of our human experience and makes it contradictory to our human nature. But if we're pulled into these two directions and it's not really where we exist, polarity is not our actual reality.

The opposite of polarity is duality. Duality is a state of having two parts in simultaneous existence. Duality is the ability to hold both things. But the question is, can we own our duality, can we have the courage to hold both things?

Duality can also be explained as the idea of everything being split in two and being able to perceive from both sides. Duality can come out in a manner that sometimes we get so associated to one side that we entirely invalidate the alternative side and when we do that when we get really entrenched that this side is right and that side is wrong, that's when we really become taken over by our own separation.

We become taken over by our egos because we're operating from a lower frequency. But there's a way to work with duality in a positive way. It's an understanding that the two sides are part of the same thing and that they actually work together and so with all things we always want to do, we should try to integrate both sides if we can find a way to do it. If you can integrate both sides, you're going to feel better and navigate through life much clearer.

Our mind is kind of split into two parts if you think about it. Carl Jung described two aspects of human nature called persona and shadow. Persona is the part of us that other people see. It's the side of you that is open for everyone to view. A shadow, however, is a part of you that contains traits of us that we don't want others to see, so we, therefore, hide or repress it. That is unconscious and we're blind to it until we make it conscious through self-analysis.

So, you have two sides and the two sides need each other. If, for example, one side of my mind decided that it was going to act independently from the other side and vice versa my reality is going to be extremely chaotic. This side is doing whatever it wants to do and the other side is also doing the same. It's very conflicting if you can imagine how having two sides of your body acting entirely independently in loathing the other side. Like if both of your eyes won't just concentrate on the same thing and hence you're not able to see a clear picture or like how if both of your legs are moving in different directions on their own and it's harder to walk.

And similarly, that's what's really going on when we look out into the world and we say this one's right and this one's wrong. It's like giving opposite ends of our body full rein to work independently which causes a great divide within us and a lot of confusion. But if we bring it back together and realize there are two sides of me and I work best when I bring these two together and work harmoniously as a unit when I appreciate both of my sides, that's when I operate at my full capacity.

It's about acknowledging your bad traits and coming with the fact that it's okay, they're there and I'll work on them, instead of just ignoring them altogether. We all have our strengths and weaknesses, and in our life, we are tested much more on our weaknesses than strengths. If you don't acknowledge or accept your other sides, our polarity might be troubling to you in most cases. Duality is holding both sides of yourself because those are the two sides that make you who you are.

—

"Life can only be understood backwards; but it must be lived forwards."

- Soren Kierkegaard

CHAPTER FOURTEEN

WHY IS IT HARD TO MEDITATE

Now, a book about acceptance and mindfulness isn't complete without the topic of meditation, is it? In this last chapter, we're here to discuss just that. However, this is not about how to meditate, this is about understanding why meditation is hard to do and why most people try it and quit before they can make it a habit.

Meditation has been scientifically proven to have many health benefits, like reduced anxiety and better emotional health. While this is great, I also see many people struggling with incorporating meditation into their daily routines. Even though it takes some effort to adopt new habits, there's one thing at play that doesn't like meditation. And that is your mind.

So, I won't deny that experienced meditators won't have too much trouble meditating whenever they want, because the wise part of their thinking mind has become dominant. However, the average person, myself included often experiences a mind that's overly active: eager to solve puzzles, analyse past events and calculate future possibilities, no matter if it's past midnight. The mind is a precious tool. But when it's out of control, it can be a destructive monster as well. The quality of our thoughts is so important because emotions are the consequence of it. As emperor and Stoic philosopher Marcus Aurelius puts it: The things you think about determining the quality of your mind. Your soul takes on the color of your thoughts.

Negative thoughts most likely cause fear, anger or grief. Positive thoughts most likely cause laughter or smiles. It's not uncommon that people that are in a constant state of negative thinking, end up being overwhelmed or anxious. The ancient practice of meditation proves to be a cure for the restless mind. The Buddhists call such a mind a monkey mind

because it tends to jump from branch to branch. Currently, health care has begun acknowledging the benefits of meditation, so we increasingly see doctors prescribing it to their patients.

The most common form of meditation is breath meditation. It's very simple, really. You just sit down or lay down, and watch the breath. You can focus on how the breath enters your nostrils, or how it fills up the lungs and belly, and you can also focus on the moments between the in and out-breath. The mind will do anything to divert your attention to the thoughts it produces. And when that happens, you focus your attention back on the breath. And when it happens again, you, again, bring back your attention to your breath.

The essence of this practice is that you don't engage with

your thinking mind, but just let it be, watch the thoughts come and go like clouds in the sky. By focusing your attention on the breath, you anchor yourself to something that is not your thinking. Even though the practice is so simple, it's incredibly difficult for many overthinkers to actually do it on a regular basis. I experience that the more active my mind is, the less I want to do it.

Especially in the evening after a busy day with lots of distractions, my thinking is often so amped up, that I'd rather scroll down the Facebook feed or watch reels and videos on YouTube than sitting down for twenty minutes watching my breath. This doesn't make sense, because checking social media and watching videos is even more tiring for an already tired mind while watching the breath gives the mind a break.

So, what's the problem? The Buddha also noticed that it's difficult to tame the mind and its restless thoughts. The struggle is, that the mind that knows that meditation is good for you, is the same mind that doesn't want to stop thinking. This part of the mind doesn't like meditation. In fact, it hates it, simply because meditation subdues its very purpose: thinking.

Now, we can make distinctions between mental states. Based on a mindfulness theory of DBT, it says that the mind is divided into three parts: the reasonable mind, the emotional mind and the wise mind. The emotional mind is a non-logical state that is dominated by emotions and creates a very subjective view of reality.

The reasonable mind operates based on facts, and is great at planning and analyzing. Both of these states, however, can be out of control. The wise mind is a healthy balance between the two; it's the part that knows what's best for you. In a state of turmoil, the little voice that knows that the mind needs a break is coming from the wise mind. The emotional mind, however, wants to be completely immersed in feelings, no matter if it's anger, grief or laughter.

And the reasonable mind wants to solve the future's problems and sort out past events and it's exhausting itself doing so. The stronger the reasonable and emotional mind is, the harder it gets to actually listen to the wise mind's voice. Meditation is a method to tame the mind, even though it doesn't want to be tamed.

That's why it's so difficult to meditate on a regular basis; it's going against the very thing that the mind enjoys doing, which is to think. Luckily, there's always a part in us that knows what's best.

The key is: listening to your mind and knowing yourself. That is what it means to be you.

—

You can follow me on Instagram and my podcast on Spotify.

For more info, you can always visit:
biru.thepurewords.com

References

Websites and Articles:

1. Freud's Model of the Human Mind | Journal Psyche. (2014). Journalpsyche.org. http://journalpsyche.org/understanding-the-human-mind/

2. Mcleod, S. (2015). Unconscious Mind | Simply Psychology. Simplypsychology.org. https://www.simplypsychology.org/unconscious-mind.html

3. Cherry, K. (2020, December 9). The Preconscious, Conscious, and Unconscious Minds. Verywell Mind; Verywellmind. https://www.verywellmind.com/the-conscious-and-unconscious-mind-2795946

4. Center, K. C. (2021, September 28). Why Do People Use Defense Mechanisms? Believe It or Not, You Used Them Too! Kentucky Counseling Center. https://kentuckycounselingcenter.com/why-do-people-use-defense-mechanisms/

5. How the Conscious Mind Was Studied by Freud. (n.d.). Verywell Mind. https://www.verywellmind.com/what-is-the-conscious-mind/

6. https://www.briantracy.com/blog/author/brian-tracy. (2017, November 15). Understanding Your Conscious Mind. Brian Tracy's Self Improvement & Professional Development Blog. https://www.briantracy.com/blog/

general/understanding-your-conscious-mind/

7. RSW, J. D. M. (2020, March 5). What Happens When We Repress Emotions? I Bhatia Psychology Group. Bhatia Psychology Group. https://bhatiapsychology.com/blog/what-happens-when-we-repress-emotions/

8. How to Regulate Your Emotions Without Suppressing Them. (n.d.). Greater Good. https://greatergood.berkeley.edu/article/item/how_to_regulate_your_emotions_without_suppressing_them

9. Repressed Emotions: Finding and Releasing Them. (n.d.). Healthline. https://www.healthline.com/health/repressed-emotions

10. Brain Dynamic Patterns and the Mind | Psychology Today. (n.d.). Www.psychologytoday.com. Retrieved December 19, 2021, from https://www.psychologytoday.com/intl/blog/the-new-science-consciousness/201703/brain-dynamic-patterns-and-the-mind

11. It's our mental patterns. (n.d.). Rlaexp.com. Retrieved December 19, 2021, from http://rlaexp.com/studio/mental_patterns.html

12. What is Sublimation? (2020, November 27). Talkspace. https://www.talkspace.com/blog/sublimation-psychology-what-is/

13. Cohen, D., & Kim, E. (2020). Sublimation (Defense Mechanism). Encyclopedia of Personality and Individual

Differences, 5275–5278. https://doi.org/10.1007/978-3-319-24612-3_1430

14. 7 Sublimation Examples in Daily Life – StudiousGuy. (n.d.). Retrieved December 19, 2021, from https://studiousguy.com/sublimation-examples/

15. Goldberg, R. (2020, August 12). The Vibration Hierarchy of Feelings. Change Your Mind Change Your Life. https://medium.com/change-your-mind/the-vibration-hierarchy-of-feelings-37b81e642bd8

16. Understanding Emotions. (2017, May 11). Shawna Freshwater, PhD. https://spacioustherapy.com/understanding-emotions/

17. How to Use the Abraham-Hicks Emotional Guidance Scale. (2020, February 2). Gabby Bernstein. https://gabbybernstein.com/emotional-guidance-scale-abraham-hicks/

18. Introversion | Psychology Today. (2019). Psychology Today. https://www.psychologytoday.com/intl/basics/introversion

19. Apparently There Are 4 Kinds of Introversion. (2020, August 11). The Cut. https://www.thecut.com/article/apparently-there-are-four-kinds-of-introversion.html

20. Introversion - an overview | ScienceDirect Topics. (n.d.). Www.sciencedirect.com. Retrieved December 19, 2021, from https://www.sciencedirect.com/topics/medicine-and-dentistry/introversion

21. Locus of Control | Simply Psychology. (n.d.). Www.simplypsychology.org. https://www.simplypsychology.org/locus-of-control.html

22. Internal Locus Of Control: Definition And Research. (n.d.). Leadership IQ. https://www.leadershipiq.com/blogs/leadershipiq/internal-locus-of-control-definition-and-research

23. Internal vs External Locus of Control: 7 Examples & Theories. (2021, August 17). PositivePsychology.com. https://positivepsychology.com/internal-external-locus-of-control/

24. Cherry, K. (2019). Locus of Control and Your Life. Verywell Mind. https://www.verywellmind.com/what-is-locus-of-control-2795434

25. The Pygmalion effect. (n.d.). The Decision Lab. https://thedecisionlab.com/biases/the-pygmalion-effect/

26. The Pygmalion Effect: Proving Them Right. (2021, May 10). Farnam Street. https://fs.blog/the-pygmalion-effect/

27. Pygmalion in Management. (2003). Harvard Business Review. https://hbr.org/2003/01/pygmalion-in-management

28. Duquesne University. (2019). The Pygmalion Effect. Duq.edu. https://www.duq.edu/about/centers-and-institutes/center-for-teaching-excellence/teaching-and-learning-at-duquesne/pygmalion

29. Duality of human nature in Dr Jekyll and Mr Hyde - Themes - AQA - GCSE English Literature Revision - AQA. (n.d.). BBC Bitesize. https://www.bbc.co.uk/bitesize/guides/z92trdm/revision/3#:~:text=Stevenson%20writes%20about%20the%20duality

30. Jain, A. (2017, July 26). The Duality of Human Nature. Medium. https://medium.com/@akashjain0708/the-duality-of-human-nature-cdc32e8adfae

31. Miller, T. C. (1993). The Duality of Human Nature. Politics and the Life Sciences, 12(2), 221–241. https://doi.org/10.1017/s0730938400024175

32. Jan 9, P. W. |, Psychology, 2012 | P., & Writing | 0 |. (n.d.). The Depth Positive Psychology of Carl Jung (Encyclopedia of Positive Psychology) | Dr. Paul Wong. Retrieved December 19, 2021, from http://www.drpaulwong.com/the-depth-positive-psychology-of-carl-jung/

33. What Makes a Man the Way He Is? (n.d.). Archive.nytimes.com. Retrieved December 19, 2021, from https://archive.nytimes.com/www.nytimes.com/books/97/09/21/reviews/jung-pyschology.html?_r=1&oref=slogin

34. The Kubrick Site: The Jungian Thing: Duality in Full Metal Jacket. (n.d.). Www.visual-Memory.co.uk. Retrieved December 19, 2021, from http://www.visual-memory.co.uk/amk/doc/0093.html

35. Mcleod, S. (2018). Carl Jung | Simply Psychology. Simplypsychology.org. https://www.simplypsychology.org/carl-jung.html

36. Carl Jung the Shadow sometimes appears as a Duality. (2020, August 5). Carl Jung Depth Psychology. https://carljungdepthpsychologysite.blog/2020/08/05/carl-jung-the-shadow-sometimes-appears-as-a-duality/#.Yb7jYPBByMo

37. Cherry, K. (2009, October 5). The 4 Major Jungian Archetypes. Verywell Mind; Verywellmind. https://www.verywellmind.com/what-are-jungs-4-major-archetypes-2795439

38. The Duality of Human Nature | What is Human Nature? (n.d.). The Diamond Net. Retrieved December 19, 2021, from https://www.thediamondnet.org/the-duality-of-human-nature-what-is-human-nature

39. Jung and his Individuation Process | Journal Psyche. (2009). Journalpsyche.org. http://journalpsyche.org/jung-and-his-individuation-process/

Video References:

1. How does the subconscious mind work? (New video). (n.d.). Www.youtube.com. Retrieved December 19, 2021, from https://www.youtube.com/watch?v=Ee2HDmbgZjc&list=LL&index=79

2. Conscious Subconscious and Superconscious Mind -

Consciousness Subconsciousness Superconsciousness. (n.d.). Www.youtube.com. Retrieved December 19, 2021, from https://www.youtube.com/watch?v=3lP07MkzyXA&list=LL&index=71&t=1s

3. Everything is Frequency and Vibration - Emotional Frequency Chart - Brain Waves (Alpha, Beta, Gamma). (n.d.). Www.youtube.com. Retrieved December 19, 2021, from https://www.youtube.com/watch?v=TdOoZLN6pZs&t=290s

4. Defense Mechanism= Sublimation. (n.d.). Www.youtube.com. Retrieved December 19, 2021, from https://www.youtube.com/watch?v=fk5jK7af1WI&t=40s

5. PSYCHOTHERAPY - Anna Freud. (n.d.). Www.youtube.com. Retrieved December 19, 2021, from https://www.youtube.com/watch?v=v80Nd8w1uts&t=190s

6. The School of Life. (2016). Freud on: Sublimation. In YouTube. https://www.youtube.com/watch?v=K96AeGqKVbs

7. What is Sublimation? (Freudian Defense Mechanism). (n.d.). Www.youtube.com. Retrieved December 19, 2021, from https://www.youtube.com/watch?v=XI1dKJ06cjA

8. How to access your unconscious mind. (n.d.). Www.youtube.com. Retrieved December 19, 2021, from https://www.youtube.com/watch?v=l9SVBN_E2fk&t=241s

9. How to Raise Your Vibration Towards ANY Subject (Higher Vibrational Manifestation). (n.d.). Www.youtube.com. Retrieved December 19, 2021, from https://www.youtube.com/watch?v=cjQfpUYwe7k&t=652s

10. Emotional spectrum. (n.d.). Www.youtube.com. Retrieved December 19, 2021, from https://www.youtube.com/watch?v=PP9u7jYqI2E

11. Einzelgänger. (2019). The Shadow Of Toxic Positivity [YouTube Video]. In YouTube. https://www.youtube.com/watch?v=VJud03V7nNA

12. The Dangers of Toxic Positivity. (n.d.). Www.youtube.com. Retrieved December 19, 2021, from https://www.youtube.com/watch?v=lAjMKHdBD3U&t=441s

13. TOXIC POSITIVITY: The Dark Side of Optimism. (n.d.). Www.youtube.com. Retrieved December 19, 2021, from https://www.youtube.com/watch?v=Ceq3Vktegyc

14. What Is Emotional Baggage? (n.d.). Www.youtube.com. Retrieved December 19, 2021, from https://www.youtube.com/watch?v=4SRc1TrJD9Q

15. Why Empaths Attract Toxic People | How to Protect Yourself | FREE COACHING GIVEAWAY. (n.d.). Www.youtube.com. Retrieved December 19, 2021, from https://www.youtube.com/watch?v=DDs2ZPDxsFg&t=167s

16. The neuroscience of imagination - Andrey Vyshedskiy. (n.d.). Www.youtube.com. Retrieved December 19, 2021, from https://www.youtube.com/watch?v=e7uXAlXdTe4&t=165s

17. How to Process Your Emotions. (n.d.). Www.youtube.com. Retrieved December 19, 2021, from https://www.youtube.com/watch?v=b197XOd9S7U&t=59s

18. What is Maladaptive Daydreaming? (n.d.). Www.youtube.com. Retrieved December 19, 2021, from https://www.youtube.com/watch?v=VxVOuCg-NG0&t=77s

19. Why Imagination Is So Important. (n.d.). Www.youtube.com. Retrieved December 19, 2021, from https://www.youtube.com/watch?v=90cfz2JHx1U&t=20s

20. The quiet power of introverts | BBC Ideas. (n.d.). Www.youtube.com. Retrieved December 19, 2021, from https://www.youtube.com/watch?v=o1Y4Z0oh1GE&t=133s

21. Our Locus of Control. (n.d.). Www.youtube.com. Retrieved December 19, 2021, from https://www.youtube.com/watch?v=l4OlctldrSU&t=16s

22. Improvement Pill. (2019). How To Stay Motivated - The Locus Rule [YouTube Video]. In YouTube. https://www.youtube.com/watch?v=8ZhoeSaPF-k

23. How to Change Your Life with The Locus Rule. (n.d.). Www.youtube.com. Retrieved December 19, 2021, from https://www.youtube.com/watch?v=YLqHGu7U9Ag&t=570s

24. What is Internal Monologue | Explained in 2 min. (n.d.). Www.youtube.com. Retrieved December 19, 2021, from https://www.youtube.com/watch?v=pEwzIcgkaoE&t=16s

25. What the What Show. (2020). What's It Like to Have No Inner Monologue? In YouTube. https://www.youtube.com/watch?v=7EIpwVHa_P8

26. The Pygmalion Effect. (2019). [YouTube Video]. In YouTube. https://www.youtube.com/watch?v=4aN5TbGW5JA

27. Why Is Meditation So Hard. (n.d.). Www.youtube.com. Retrieved December 19, 2021, from https://www.youtube.com/watch?v=LrwM3JNm4BU&t=153s

28. What is DUALITY? A very simple explanation! (n.d.). Www.youtube.com. Retrieved December 19, 2021, from https://www.youtube.com/watch?v=bxa8yg0T2X0

29. Understanding Duality - Part 1 - Master List of 250+ Dualities. (n.d.). Www.youtube.com. Retrieved December 19, 2021, from https://www.youtube.com/watch?v=FO3YtZwhN2k&t=2936s

30. Hopeless Duality Of Man. (n.d.). Www.youtube.com.

Retrieved December 19, 2021, from https://www.youtube.com/watch?v=cF0ISsHf-T8&t=36s

31. Duality: An English Unit - Lesson 03 - The Philosophy of Duality. (n.d.). Www.youtube.com. Retrieved December 19, 2021, from https://www.youtube.com/watch?v=VO63162Npa8&t=263s

9 798885 460668

Printed by Libri Plureos GmbH in Hamburg, Germany